Astrology

Astrology

Understanding Your Star Sign

TRADITIONAL CHINESE BOOKBINDING
This book has been produced using traditional Chinese bookbinding techniques, using a
method that was developed during the Ming Dynasty (1368–1644) and remained in use until
the adoption of Western binding techniques in the early 1900s. In traditional Chinese binding,
single sheets of paper are printed on one side only, and each sheet is folded in half, with the
printed pages on the outside. The book block is then sandwiched between two boards and
sewn together through punched holes close to the cut edges of the folded sheets.

Contents

Introduction

Every man, woman and child is born with a distinct and different destiny. There are no exceptions. Everyone, no matter how humble, has cosmic significance and a part to play in the life of the universe. This is innate and inescapable, and goes beyond the tiny boundaries of nation, creed and colour.

As we live out our lives, we are, however unknowingly, acting in a greater drama and reacting to impulses that come from distant astronomical bodies, stars and planets millions of light years away. Sceptics pour scorn on the idea that far-distant Saturn, for example, could have any effect on our lives, as the ancient art and science of astrology teaches. But we are sparks of energy inhabiting bodies made of the same stuff as the stars, responding like tiny radios to the distant messages that they send to Earth.

Each infant carries within it a double blueprint for life: its genetic programming and the pattern of character that comes from the astrological 'clock' that was set in motion at the moment of birth. No one knows the full extent of genetic influence, although it seems to be astonishingly far-reaching, but the power of the horoscope has been well known to the wisest men and women for many, many centuries.

Our Sun and Moon signs provide essential inside information about our destinies. They reveal the secrets of who we really are, and why we are here, laying out before us our potential, the sort of joys and achievements our characteristics may bring about, and warn us of problems to be overcome through the triumph of free will.

Read *Astrology* with an open mind and discover who you really are.

Finding Your Sun Sign

Aries
21 March – 20 April

Taurus
21 April – 21 May

Gemini
22 May – 21 June

Cancer
22 June – 22 July

Leo
23 July – 23 August

Virgo
24 August – 22 September

Libra
23 September – 23 October

Scorpio
24 October – 22 November

Sagittarius
23 November – 21 December

Capricorn
22 December – 20 January

Aquarius
21 January – 18 February

Pisces
19 February – 20 March

The Elements

U p to the beginning of the Age of Enlightenment in the 18th century, it was commonly believed that everything, including human beings, was made up of the four elements: Earth, Air, Fire and Water. These were thought of as the building blocks of life, and each astrological sign had a predominance of one or another. Each created its common characteristics, although too much of any of the elements can produce an unbalanced personality.

EARTH SIGNS

The signs ruled by Earth are Taurus, Virgo and Capricorn. Each manifests the element in different ways. However, in all cases, Earth makes those born under these signs more practical, sensible and stable than most. They are more grounded. For example, Arians may be the great explorers and adventurers of the zodiac, but it is Taureans who follow behind, set up camp for them and arrange provisions. Organized Virgoans are the analysts and note keepers who keep track of records and archives so that society knows its history. Capricornians always have an eye to the future, planning ahead for a rainy day from their lofty mountain peaks, like the Goat that symbolizes their sign.

WATER SIGNS

The Water Signs are Cancer, Scorpio and Pisces. They are emotional, intuitive and often psychic, strongly in touch with the hidden, mysterious side of life. Like the ocean tides, they have surges of inspiration and bursts of euphoria, or they can be plunged into gloom and introspection.

Cancerians are emotionally tied to their homes and families. Scorpians are the occultists and profound thinkers of the zodiac, very sexy and magnetic, but sometimes too intense. Pisceans' emotions can lie undisturbed for long periods, then suddenly rise to the surface. They can be fast and elusive and change direction for no apparent reason.

AIR SIGNS

The Air Signs are Gemini, Libra and Aquarius. These inspirational, communicative signs of the zodiac can talk a great deal of 'hot air', and their ability to cause a 'wind of change' to run through society is a mixed blessing. Often the Air Signs are blown this way and that by sudden enthusiasms and contradictory opinions, but they can throw new light on apparently intractable problems. Geminians talk and act fast, and live life at a furious pace. Librans are calm and collected, the arbiters and diplomats of the zodiac. Aquarians, the idealists, can move swiftly if their crusading zeal is fully engaged, and their motivation is razor-sharp. If they feel something is best for humankind, they will go for it.

FIRE SIGNS

The Fire Signs are Aries, Leo and Sagittarius. Consumed with passion – which all too often, however, takes the form of self-love and burning ambition – these are the natural stars of the zodiac. Fire Signs are the leaders – especially Leo, King of the Jungle, the most imperious of all the signs of the zodiac. Arians can burn with a cold flame or with the raging fires of revolution. Either way, their passion is based on a childlike desire to get their own way. But without them human progress would always be a great deal slower and more difficult. Sagittarians are the great enthusiasts of the zodiac.

Planets

Until the 18th century, astrologers knew only the planets of our solar system that could be seen with the naked eye: Mercury, Venus, Mars, Jupiter and Saturn. (For the purposes of astrology, the Sun and the Moon are also counted as planets even though the Sun is a star and the Moon is the satellite of Earth.) Uranus was discovered in 1781, Neptune in 1846 and Pluto was first seen in 1930.

THE SUN

The Sun, around which nine planets and their satellites revolve, is the life-giver of our solar system. Many ancient civilizations worshipped the Sun. Zeus, Helios, Mithras, Ra, Atum and Aten were just some of the many Sun gods who were venerated millennia ago. Gold and kingship are associated with the Sun, the ruler of Leo and archetypical sign of nobility and worldly achievement. Its fire inspires loyalty and ambition. However, Sun-subjects can be ruthless and overbearing, and their fire can die very quickly, leaving them lazy and downcast. The day that was originally sacred to the Sun was, of course, Sunday.

THE MOON

The Moon has a major role to play in the drama of life on Earth. It causes tides to ebb and flow, and induces certain types of behaviour in animals – many animals become restless under a Full Moon. Research strongly suggests that humans are similarly affected. In mythology, the Moon is traditionally associated with women, with magic and seduction, whereas the Sun is honoured as a very male god. Cancerians are ruled by the Moon, which is believed to make them emotional, caring and nurturing, although they can become easily distressed and possessive. The sacred day of the Moon is Monday.

VENUS

Venus has always been associated with beauty, harmony and love. The name comes from the Roman goddess of love, who also governed clothes, finery and luxury. The negative side of Venus is expressed in venereal diseases, which were once thought to be caused by an excess of Venusian influence. Venus rules both Taurus and Libra, endowing them with an appreciation of beautiful things and a love of sex. Both, in their own way, seek harmony – Taureans, with their need for stability, while Librans' distaste for confrontation underscores all their relationships. The sacred day of Venus is Friday.

MERCURY

Mercury was the name of the Roman messenger god, ruler of communication, whose great energy always kept him on the move. All the mercurial gods share the same dual nature. They are both trickster and friend of the human race. Gemini and Virgo are both ruled by Mercury. Typical Geminians are truly mercurial – quick-witted, fast talkers, energetic and volatile. However, there can also be an element of the trickster in them. Virgoans are great communicators but at a slower pace. They think before they speak and can be immensely entertaining. The sacred day of Mercury is Wednesday.

MARS

Mars was the Roman god of war, from whom we derive our word 'martial'. Arians are ruled by war-like Mars, as are Scorpians (although the latter are now also ruled by Pluto). Mars gives Aries its fiery zeal, courage that

often amounts to foolhardiness and its explosive temper. It bestows on
Scorpio its red-blooded sense of drama and angry passion. Tuesday is
sacred to Mars.

JUPITER

Jupiter was the Greco-Roman god of plenty, also known as Jove or, in
ancient Greece, Zeus. Traditionally deemed a 'lucky' planet by astrologers,
Jupiter is the ruler of Sagittarius, and is associated with joy, plenty,
philosophy and all manner of academic study. Happy-go-lucky and naturally
disposed to be optimistic, Sagittarians do seem to embody the air of
cheerful expectancy conjured up by Jupiter. They accept that anything can
happen but have little fear for the future, feeling instinctively that fate will
take care of them. Jupiter's sacred day is Thursday.

SATURN

The god Saturn originally governed the agricultural arts, but later he gave
his name to the Roman festival of Saturnalia, in which the dark of winter
was enlivened with music, feasting and more than a little lechery. This
usually took place at the winter solstice of 20–21 December.

Saturn rules Capricorn (and, more controversially, Aquarius). It can
bring restrictions in its wake, and can make its subjects inclined to be
narrow in outlook. However, it is also the bringer of tenacity and the
wisdom that comes from learning the hard way. The day sacred to Saturn is,
of course, Saturday.

URANUS

In Greek mythology, Uranus was the son of the Great Mother, from whose
incestuous mating were born all the creatures of the Earth. Uranus is

associated with abrupt upheaval. His rulership of sudden change highlights the impermanence of life and the way in which all of Man's greatest achievements and material wealth can be swept away. Astrologically, Uranus governs Aquarius, bestowing the ability to be original and idealistic. The negative aspects of Uranus as a ruling planet are its tendency to make Aquarians too eager to sweep away the old and to seek 'kicks' in dangerous ways. Uranus has no sacred day.

NEPTUNE

Neptune was the Roman version of the Greek god of the sea, Poseidon. Astrologically, Neptune is associated with artistic expression and illusion. The planet can encourage fine creativity, but at the same time mislead the unwary into dead-end activities such as gambling. Pisceans, the dreamy, indecisive and sometimes even deceitful sign, reflect Neptune's curious power. There is an element of insubstantial promises about Neptune, like wishes in fairy stories. They may come true, but in a cruelly deceptive way. Neptune has no sacred day but, associated with the Moon, which rules the sea, Monday may be considered a suitable candidate.

PLUTO

Pluto was named after the ancient Greco-Roman god Pluto, who ruled the Underworld. He was associated with dread, inevitability and doom. Astrologically, Pluto is associated with the dark, unconscious mind, with secrets and karmic liabilities. With Mars, the ninth planet now co-rules Scorpio, endowing that sign with its passion for the occult and for plumbing the depths of the human psyche. There is no day sacred to Pluto but, by association with Mars, Tuesday could be eligible. Saturday, the day of Saturn, is also a contender.

The Genders

Traditionally, the 12 signs of the zodiac are divided into masculine and feminine, although of course both men and women are born into each.

The characteristics were assigned to the genders aeons ago and may now seem old-fashioned. However, the signs do seem to be grouped according to the appropriate gender.

MASCULINE SIGNS

The Masculine signs are Aries, Gemini, Leo, Libra, Sagittarius and Aquarius. Masculine traits do tend to be accentuated in the Fire signs, which are Aries, Leo and Sagittarius.

Masculine signs are dominant and assertive, often to the point of being pugnacious, and extroverted. They are natural leaders and rulers, showing fiery initiative and are fiercely protective of others in their care. They are pioneers and visionaries, conquerors of new lands and the first to achieve great things. They tend to tackle things themselves and can be impatient with others who are less assertive.

Negatively, Masculine signs can be egotistical, arrogant and cruel, and dismissive of the needs and feelings of others. They can be troublemakers and rebels – violent, belligerent and inclined to subversion.

FEMININE SIGNS

The Feminine signs are Taurus, Cancer, Virgo, Scorpio, Capricorn and Pisces. Feminine traits tend to be accentuated in the Water signs Cancer and Pisces.

These signs present gentler, more passive qualities. They are the carers and the nurturers, inclined to take a back seat and worry over the wellbeing of others. They are artistic and in tune with their intuition, and may be psychic. Self-evidently, these are the motherly, sisterly, signs, with all the attendant positive and negative characteristics. They tend to be the power behind the throne, rather than movers and shakers, although many are great achievers, especially in the modern, more egalitarian world, where their qualities are encouraged.

Negatively, the Feminine signs can be fussy, possessive, mean-minded, vindictive, clinging and over-emotional.

Aquarius, the sign of the coming Age, is endowed with both Masculine and Feminine traits, although it is traditionally categorized as Masculine.

The Qualities

In addition to the influence of gender, the elements and the planets, each sign of the zodiac is affected by having an intrinsic quality which is Cardinal, Fixed or Mutable. These qualities represent three fundamentals in life: Cardinal for creation, Fixed for preservation and Mutable for adjustment. Each quality influences four of the zodiac signs.

CARDINAL

Those with a strong Cardinal quality to their chart are, traditionally, supremely ambitious and perhaps somewhat ruthless in getting to the top. Their sense of determination inspires others, although they themselves will continue to take the lead and initiate every new project. Cardinality also represents new beginnings.

ARIES

Arians are volcanic in their desire to get ahead and will not stand for any opposition. Energetic, forceful and competitive, they rush headlong towards their goal and are not above skulduggery to get their own way.

CANCER

Unassertive and introverted, many Cancerians can still be courageous and determined fighters, although usually on behalf of others, especially their children.

Libra

Many Librans use their pleasant, 'anything for a quiet life' manner in order to achieve their ambitions, for example lulling potential rivals into a false sense of security. They can be surprisingly assertive and ambitious.

Capricorn

Like the Goat of their sign, Capricornians will react with fury if anyone attempts to dominate them. There will come a point when they erupt, put their heads down – and charge! They also harbour strong, long-term ambitions. Many Capricornians are not happy in a competitive situation and will do anything to end it – but only by winning.

Fixed

Individuals born under a Fixed sign have an inherent disposition towards tradition, convention and stability. They hate change and often refuse to adapt to new circumstances. These people are not happy taking the initiative or being in situations that require a quick-fire response. Fixed signs also tend to have conventional, conservative opinions and find it hard to move with the times.

Taurus

Strong and stubborn, Taureans are the people who translate the great plans of others into solid reality. They are at ease with customs and have great respect for old-fashioned values. They are loyal and unhappy with any challenge to the status quo.

Leo

Those born under the sign of the Lion believe that they have a natural nobility and that they are leaders of men. Their innate laziness, however, makes them disinclined to stir from any comfortable situation, be it a job, a life partnership or a home. They hate change for its own sake and, despite their ambition, lack the necessary stamina to fight their rivals to the bitter end.

Scorpio

Although highly emotional, those born under this Water Sign know their own mind and react strongly against challenges to their position. Often unable to adapt or see alternative points of view, Scorpians take everything very personally.

Aquarius

At first sight, this progressive, idealistic sign would seem to be the antithesis of Fixed. However, many Aquarians are remarkably set in their ways, even though those ways may seem unorthodox.

Mutable

Those born under the Mutable signs are always on the move, either physically or mentally. They are restless, versatile and flexible, hating routine and any form of strict discipline.

GEMINI

Creative and persuasive, Geminians personify Mutable qualities. They loathe restriction of any kind. Forever seizing on the main chance, they are articulate and can be very amusing. Extremely gregarious, they are unhappy alone or in an unchanging environment.

VIRGO

Excellent communicators, Virgoans make pleasant companions, revealing a sharp wit and a sense of the absurd. However, their Mutable qualities are tempered by being an Earth Sign, which restrains their flights of fancy and makes them essentially realistic.

SAGITTARIUS

Always on the move, always with an eye to the next project, lover or ambition, Sagittarians are very Mutable individuals. They become unhappy, sometimes to the point of becoming ill, if they are expected to conform. Sagittarians are delightful people with unbounded energy and a relentless curiosity about life, but they frequently lack the energy necessary to follow projects through to their conclusion.

PISCES

Emotional, insecure Pisceans are creative and intuitive, but often seem a little adrift in the everyday world. They seek peace, harmony and love, and can tend to have an unrealistic view of life. In some cases, this is all that gets them through, because a negative side of this sign is the ease with which Pisceans lose incentive and take refuge in illusion.

SUN SIGNS

Sun Signs

Your Sun Sign determines your personality, whereas your Moon Sign influences your inner mood and emotions. It is easy to determine your Sun Sign from the day and month of your birth. In the pages that follow, you will discover the major characteristics of all the Sun Signs, along with, more specifically, how each Sun Sign differs in three main areas: the kind of worker they are, how they behave in friendships and relationships, and which other Sun Sign is most compatible with them as a life partner.

ARIES

21 March – 20 April

Sun Sign: ARIES

Sign: THE RAM

Ruling Planet: MARS

Gender: MASCULINE

Element: FIRE

Quality: CARDINAL

Colour: RED

Birthstones: DIAMOND, HELIOTROPE

Compatibility: TAURUS AND VIRGO

Non-compatibility: LEO, GEMINI, LIBRA AND AQUARIUS

The Sun In Aries

Sun Sign Arians are feisty, straightforward and adventurous. Blessed with abundant energy and drive, they have no time for laziness or prevarication and make excellent motivators whether in the workplace or at home. Keen-witted, they see straight to the heart of a problem, cutting away all the unnecessary distractions.

The first sign of the zodiac, Aries represents springtime, the burgeoning of new life. There is a childlike belief in miracles, in things coming right. Often, though, this blind faith is justified. Positively aspected Arians can be very lucky. There is an attractive naivety about them, and an ability to find energy and resources inside themselves when everyone around them is burned out.

Negative Arian characteristics arise out of their driven nature. Often, they seem cold and afflicted with tunnel vision. To them, the end usually justifies the means, even if the way to the top involves methods that are questionable, or even ruthless. They are childishly egocentric, always leaping before giving even the most cursory look around. As a consequence, they often find themselves in deep trouble.

They are disarmingly frank, and in their eagerness to let everyone know exactly where they stand they can be very hurtful. They are good with words but all too often they use them as weapons and can be cuttingly sarcastic and dismissive. Profoundly self-centred, they rarely bother to see themselves as others see them and this is the hardest lesson for them to learn.

Career

Their energy and disregard for their own safety or comfort makes Arians pioneers at heart. Anything involving long-term planning is anathema to Arians, and moneymaking is usually incidental to their ambitions. Typical Arians are better at making money for others than for themselves. They are ill at ease with repetitive jobs, seeking to express themselves as individuals whenever possible. They thrive on challenges, and have an enviable capacity to concentrate on the job in hand.

Relationships

Passionate and incurably romantic, Arians tend to need joyous sex and close relationships throughout their lives. Rows will be frequent and, always demanding, all Arians will expect, rather than give, support. Under their pomposity and bluster, they can often be very vulnerable, and the wise partner soon realizes that they need to be encouraged and praised constantly. Although they will love their spouses, parents and family devotedly, everything begins and ends with their perspective.

Ideal Partner

Arians need support, encouragement and bringing down to earth, so their ideal life partner belongs to one of the Earth signs, Taurus or Virgo. Their ruling planet, Venus, is the perfect counter to Martian extremism, softening a tendency to see life as a series of all-or-nothing challenges. Taureans are restrained, no-nonsense individuals who often have a secret admiration for flamboyant Arians. Virgoans can be considerably more organized than Arians; however, their introversion can irritate the average Arian.

COMPATIBILITY

Aries
Fire meets fire with fellow Arians, and a clash of egos may cause far too many problems for a happy life.

Cancer
Home-loving Cancerians may offer stability but cause too many scenes. Sometimes it works, though.

Libra
Gregarious and fun-loving Librans can suit Arians, but the Ram's ambitions can be too self-centred.

Capricorn
Repressed, inhibited Goats may hero-worship Arians but this combination won't last for long.

Taurus
Calm, dignified and stolid Taureans can give madcap Arians the status and stable home they seek.

Leo
Two volatile Fire Signs together do not make for a happy life. Some Leos are big enough to compromise.

Scorpio
Aries will be fascinated by the deep, unfathomable Scorpian but life will prove too intense for comfort.

Aquarius
Crusading Aquarians can all too often succeed in clashing with pioneering Arians for the centre of attention.

Gemini
Geminians tend to be too flighty – and often too wily – for pioneering Arians' long-term plans.

Virgo
Orderly, down-to-earth Virgoans can ideally complement Arian fire, as long as they are not too secretive.

Sagittarius
Arians and easy-going Sagittarians do get on but in the end both will go their separate ways.

Pisces
Dreamy and emotional Pisceans will often find it hard to give Arians the emotional freedom they need.

TAURUS

21 April – 21 May

Sun Sign: TAURUS

Sign: THE BULL

Ruling Planet: VENUS

Gender: FEMININE

Element: EARTH

Quality: FIXED

Colour: GREEN

Birthstone: EMERALD

Compatibility: ARIES, TAURUS AND SCORPIO

Non-compatibility: AQUARIUS AND SAGITTARIUS

The Sun In Taurus

un Sign Taureans are reliable, responsible and affectionate, with strong artistic leanings and a winning way with money. Taureans prefer to stick to well-established plans, rather than change or adapt, and are excellent homemakers and builders of secure families. They are patient, determined and possessed of enormous reserves of strength and common sense. The 'salt of the earth' and strangers to Arian-style tantrums or impulsiveness, they are towers of strength in a crisis. Taureans love routine and rarely question rules and regulations, possessing a natural inclination to respect authority and take orders. Excellent seconds-in-command, they do not often aspire to be the top of their chosen profession.

Warm-hearted and loving people, Taureans seek above all to create a happy family. Their home is always their castle. One of their most negative traits is indolence, the ability to switch off and do absolutely nothing, except perhaps eat, drink and make love.

The sensualists par excellence of the zodiac, Taureans can turn being pampered into a serious art form. They love being touched, and can suffer real feelings of deprivation if denied the joys of love.

Taureans are also liable to fierce possessiveness and to making unreasonable accusations, seeing serious liaisons in the most light-hearted and innocent of banter. Mostly, however, Taurean negativity is expressed in dullness, stubbornness and resistance to change. Taureans can be 'Old Fogeys' at any age.

CAREER

Intensely practical people, Sun Sign Taureans are happiest when creating something tangible and lasting, be it a house, garden or painting. A fixed Earth sign, they are good at putting down roots and maintaining their stability against the ravages of change. Methodical, thorough and punctual though they may be, Taureans are often content to sit out their entire working lives in dull jobs, never seriously going for promotion or moving to something more challenging and rewarding.

RELATIONSHIPS

Conscientious and dutiful, Taureans don't like spontaneity and do like to know where they stand, so that they can carve out a distinctive role for themselves that will last, unchanging, throughout the years. They seek harmony, but can suffer real emotional hardship just to keep the peace. Homemakers and home-lovers, they are always hospitable entertainers but sometimes are disinclined to venture forth, even on family get-togethers or holidays, which can prove testing for non-Taurean partners.

IDEAL PARTNER

Taureans who seek emotional and material stability could do a lot worse than spend their lives with another Taurean, although sparks will fly should both these obstinate natures clash. They are inclined to be faithful and carry the same values throughout life, and so can make a perfect, if not the most stimulating, match. If Taureans want a little magic in their lives, they should go for their opposite sign – the intense, magnetic Scorpio.

COMPATIBILITY

Aries
Dashing Arians add sparkle to the life of the more prosaic Taurean. They can have long, successful relationships.

Cancer
Well-behaved, stolid, reserved Taureans can find Cancerian scenes just too much to take – but can learn to cope.

Libra
Librans, also ruled by Venus, seriously attract Taureans. Librans' outlook is too cool, though.

Capricorn
The unadventurous Goat can find happiness with a stolid Bull but sooner or later a red rag will appear.

Taurus
Fellow Taureans make for safety, convention and stability. This can work but it won't be very exciting.

Leo
Egocentric Leos often charm Taureans but sooner or later there will be a huge, disastrous – and final – showdown.

Scorpio
Opposite sign Scorpians fascinate Taureans but there may be too much murkiness for convention-bound Taureans.

Aquarius
To Taureans, unconventional Aquarians can often seem to have come from another planet. No chance!

Gemini
Taureans are often attracted to easy-going and sociable Geminians, who can be too daring for this to last.

Virgo
Earthy and very organized Virgoans attract Taurean but this combination can prove too predictable for both.

Sagittarius
All that energy and irresponsibility charm but ultimately horrify steady Taureans, who prefer pensions to penury.

Pisces
Excessively emotional, clingy Pisceans can be a very definite turn-off for salt-of-the-earth Taureans.

GEMINI

22 May – 21 June

Sun Sign: GEMINI

Sign: THE TWINS

Ruling Planet: MERCURY

Gender: MASCULINE

Element: AIR

Quality: MUTABLE

Colours: YELLOW OR GOLD

Birthstones: PEARL, MOONSTONE

Compatibility: AQUARIUS

Non-compatibility: TAURUS, CAPRICORN AND VIRGO

The Sun In Gemini

Sun Sign Geminians tend to be jacks of all trades and masters of none – or at least few. Quick-witted and versatile, they love wordplay and jokes, and are often extremely witty and amusing companions. Expert communicators, they are confident public speakers with enviable timing and panache, and are excellent at networking or bringing shy or diverse people together in social situations.

However, even though Geminians are noted for mental fluency, they can suffer from a very short attention span and routine scares them away.

As for living alone, it's simply not on the agenda. A Geminian must have an audience or at least someone else to bounce ideas off – and, hopefully, someone who occasionally has the good sense to bring them down to earth.

Their major flaws are superficiality and manipulativeness. Ruled by Mercury, their quicksilver minds rarely alight on any one subject long enough to absorb the finer points. They can also be very guileful, sometimes to the point of being accomplished liars. The tricksters of the zodiac, Geminians are constantly looking for the main chance, regardless of the cost in human terms. They are frequently cold-hearted and uneasy with the gentler emotions. The fact is that Geminians are very uncomfortable with deep emotions, and when faced with strong feelings they tend to take refuge in flippant remarks, sarcasm or logical analysis. Their inconsistency has given rise to the interpretation of the sign of the Twins as being 'two-faced'.

Career

Although many Geminians are successfully self-employed, they find working alone absolutely unacceptable because they need the motivation and feedback of a workplace. The ultimate charmers and communicators, typical Geminians are the salespersons of the zodiac. They enjoy challenges, but feel trapped by deadly routine or too many rules and regulations. Anything that involves using personality and persuasion suits Geminians, though that can include the life of a confidence trickster.

Relationships

Geminians enjoy being in a lively family and seek partners with strong opinions and marked preferences – at least it's something to discuss and argue over. Talking is always the Geminian's favourite hobby; listening has to be an acquired skill. Many Geminians have relatively few real friends but dozens of acquaintances. They are keen to make relationships work but tend to be too egocentric and outgoing to ever really know what makes their partners tick, or why they are unhappy.

Ideal Partner

Because they often have their head in the clouds, Geminians need a planner, someone who is careful with money. Taureans are too plodding and Capricornians far too pessimistic, but typical Sun Sign Virgoans, though they can be far too analytical and organized, can do the trick if softened with other planetary influences. Perhaps, curiously, it is another air sign – Aquarius – that is ideal for them. Aquarians understand the Geminian restlessness and drive, but add their own gentleness and more profound idealism.

COMPATIBILITY

Aries
Feisty Arians may seem glamorous but underneath they are far too serious and self-focused for Geminians.

Cancer
Cancerian emotional blackmail and frequent tantrums will send Gemini fleeing. Calmer Crabs might last.

Libra
Both real charmers, Geminians and Librans can seem to have something special but they won't be soul mates.

Capricorn
The austere Goat may view easy-going and plausible Geminians with suspicion and – justifiable – cynicism.

Taurus
Taureans all too often fall for the famous Geminian charm, which will finally be too superficial for the heavyweight Bull.

Leo
High and mighty Leos can be magnificent lovers but, all too often, there will be a major personality clash.

Scorpio
Scorpians' glamour will fascinate Geminians and there may be a real sexual buzz, but tears in the end.

Aquarius
Geminians can fall for the challenge of life with a true Aquarian in a big way and find lifelong happiness.

Gemini
Fellow Geminians know only too well each other's wiles – so this won't usually work for long.

Virgo
Geminians can find the more sociable Virgoans good company but they will soon tire of them.

Sagittarius
This will be a fun relationship with wild times and big plans but it won't make for a settled, cosy home.

Pisces
Geminians have little patience for the often difficult, emotionally intense and rather contradictory Pisceans.

CANCER

22 June – 22 July

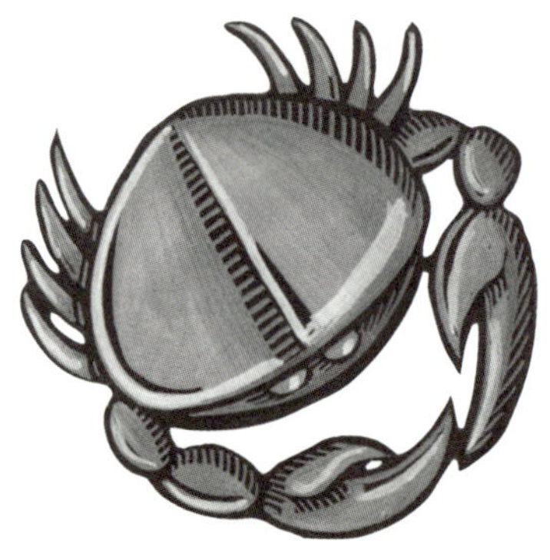

Sun Sign: CANCER

Sign: THE CRAB

Ruling Planet: THE MOON

Gender: FEMININE

Element: WATER

Quality: CARDINAL

Colours: PALE BLUE AND SILVER

Birthstone: RUBY

Compatibility: TAURUS AND WELL-ASPECTED LEOS

Non-compatibility: CAPRICORN AND PISCES

The Sun In Cancer

un Sign Cancerians are the most family-centred of the zodiac. Fiercely protective of their loved ones, they are nourishers and carers at heart. Cancerians are also in tune with their true self and in touch with their intuition. They can be intuitively wise, but distrust cold logic and analysis. Though often without driving ambition for themselves, they yearn passionately on behalf of others. They are artistic, practical and excellent homemakers. The world outside rarely offers anything to eclipse the attraction of coming home, especially home to the family, and even lone Cancerians lavish time and money on creating their ideal.

However, those born under the sign of the Crab are great worriers, constantly fretting about the health and safety of their family and friends. This can test their relationships. Also, they take offence easily. They tend to fall out with others and subsequently keep their distance, often for years.

Cancerians are nothing if not tenacious. They hang on to a relationship, belief or cause with their crab's claws, even when it causes them pain. For them, it is enormously difficult to let go and move on.

Being highly emotional makes Cancerians moody, withdrawn and even secretive. Sometimes they can sulk for days, without being able to find out why. They are both loving and loyal, but can be unsure of themselves and somewhat timid socially, preferring to give someone else the limelight.

Career

Being naturally sympathetic, practical and nurturing, Cancerians are drawn to roles in education, counselling and healthcare. Reliable and responsible, they make good co-workers but they can equally run their own small businesses. This is where being so organized with money helps. Cancerians also make imaginative cooks, although they prefer to see people's reactions to their dishes, rather than remaining behind the scenes in the kitchen.

Relationships

Cancerians make loving parents, sensitive lovers and generally docile children. However, they can be overprotective of their own children. They cling: long after any hope of reconciliation in a former relationship, Cancerians are still trying to revive the long-dead embers. Many Cancerians do not realize that they have the power to lash out and hurt others. When blinded by emotion, they will never see reason. They take every little criticism personally, and brood over it, possibly even for years.

Ideal Partner

Cancerians should stay clear of typical Sun Signs who cannot cope with emotions. Best for them are steady, grounded types such as Taureans, who can be very happy to create a nest with these traditional homebodies. They also understand the need to keep a firm hand on the bank balance, and this combination creates an almost ideally secure background in which their children can grow up and fulfil their real potential.

COMPATIBILITY

Aries
The fire and dash of Aries appeals but they have little time for Cancerian emotion. It might work – but not for long.

Cancer
Although they have much in common, two emotional blackmailers under the same roof can make for disaster.

Libra
Life can be easy for a while, but Librans value their independence too much to hand it over to a Cancerian.

Capricorn
True Goats will never understand the Cancerian's need to discuss emotion, which will frighten them off for good.

Taurus
This is the perfect match: both are homemakers and respecters of family values. They will enhance each other's life.

Leo
Cancerians can worship Leos and make fine homes with them. With enough compromise, this can be an excellent match.

Scorpio
Flashy Scorpians may infatuate Cancerians, but the price is too high. One drama queen is enough!

Aquarius
Home-loving Cancerians feel threatened by crusading Aquarians who want to change their settled world.

Gemini
Self-seeking Geminians can be charm itself, but they will never be a lifelong partner.

Virgo
This combination can work, though Virgoans may be puzzled and upset by Cancerian outbursts and contradictions.

Sagittarius
Cancerians want to own their beloved's body and soul – the last thing a Sagittarian will ever agree to.

Pisces
Both Water Signs can be tearful clingers, which is not the best recipe for lasting love or mutual respect.

LEO

23 July – 23 August

Sun Sign: LEO

Sign: THE LION

Ruling Planet: THE SUN

Gender: MASCULINE

Element: FIRE

Quality: FIXED

Colours: GOLD AND YELLOW-ORANGE

Birthstones: PERIDOT, ONYX

Compatibility: CANCER, AQUARIUS AND VIRGO

Non-compatibility: SCORPIO AND GEMINI

The Sun In Leo

Sun Sign Leos are powerful, ambitious, and protective – truly the kings of the jungle. Ruled by the Sun, they are outgoing and optimistic, their sunny disposition often inspiring lesser mortals. They are the party animals of the zodiac, dynamic and uninhibited, believing that they can achieve whatever they set out to. Warm-hearted and often extremely generous, they love company – especially if they are the centre of attention. Well-aspected Sun Sign Leos are intrinsically faithful partners and loyal friends, and extremely loving in a very expansive way. When life is good for a Leo, everyone in their circle benefits.

Conversely, when Leos are crossed and their integrity or self-esteem is challenged, they can fly into towering rages. These may soon evaporate, but they can leave those at the receiving end shaken. It is easy for Leos to become overbearing. Sometimes they seem to demand worship from those closest to them, without realizing that respect must be earned. Some Leos are bullies, taking advantage of any weakness in others, while many can be domineering and unapproachable. They can also be extremely dogmatic and ruthless in pursuing their particular ideology, giving no thought to the beliefs of others.

Even Leos who appear to be quiet and restrained have all the virtues and flaws of the typical, expansive Lion. If you want to see Leos turn from pussycat into magnificent, terrifying king of the jungle, just injure their pride or treat them with contempt. Then the seemingly docile tabby shakes out its mane and growls.

Career

Leos are happiest and most effective in any career where they can give orders or be the centre of attention. Being second-in-command or a humble team member is not for them. Whatever they do, they expect their attention to be fully engaged, and to be constantly praised and given positive feedback. They can't do any job for long, especially something routine or tedious, without bursting out and opting for something that offers to fulfil their considerable potential.

Relationships

Leos make wonderfully sociable companions, amusing and urbane. They tend to have a large circle of friends, many of them close and many for life. They rarely live alone and are usually fairly easy to live with, although they do expect others to live up to their own high standards as they cannot tolerate failure. Though Leos are passionate lovers, they can still look elsewhere if their partners injure their over-developed sense of pride.

Ideal Partner

As long as they are fully supported and loved, Leos can conduct a successful relationship with almost any sign. They can make a happy lifelong commitment to the emotional and home-loving Cancerian or the supportive, stable Taurean. There will, of course, be problems, for Leos always expect primacy and deference, and even the most martyrly Cancerian will sometimes feel slighted by this situation. Gentle, idealistic Aquarians can cope better with Leo's excessive demands, although they may not always be there when needed.

COMPATIBILITY

Aries
Matching fire with fire – and ego with ego – is not a good recipe for a harmonious and loving relationship.

Cancer
This is an enviable partnership: more well-balanced Cancerians can make a happy nest with a beloved Leo.

Libra
Librans and Leos are mutually attracted but the Scales dither too much for decisive, opinionated Leo.

Capricorn
Any initial attraction will soon wear thin due to the Goat's innate distrust of Leonine extravagance.

Taurus
Steady, feet-on-the-ground Taureans can make it work with Leos but, too often, there will be a spark missing.

Leo
There can never be two kings in the same jungle. One will be forced to back off or submit. Not a happy pairing.

Scorpio
There will be great sex and memorable times but the intensity will cause too many problems in the long term.

Aquarius
Leos can make a go of it with big-thinking Aquarians, but they may need more support than is forthcoming.

Gemini
Good times will be enjoyed, but difficult-to-pin-down Geminians will not provide Leo with the right kind of home life.

Virgo
More relaxed Virgoans can hit it off fairly well with expansive Leos, but most are too inhibited to try.

Sagittarius
All fire and energy, these two will wear each other out with their headlong rush at life and fierce power struggles.

Pisces
This combination makes for a rollercoaster partnership. The water, in this case, is more likely to put out the fire.

VIRGO

24 August – 22 September

Sun Sign: Virgo

Sign: The Virgin

Ruling Planet: Mercury

Gender: Feminine

Element: Earth

Quality: Mutable

Colour: Brown-Red

Birthstone: Sapphire

Compatibility: Pisces and some Aquarians

Non-compatibility: Leo and Sagittarius

The Sun In Virgo

Sun Sign Virgoans are not necessarily virginal, of course, but they often have the quiet, unsophisticated air of an inexperienced person, which can be deceptive. They are meticulous, tidy and thorough. Typical Sun Sign Virgoans keep their own counsel, and although they are frequently profound thinkers, they are essentially practical. These enormously hard-working people are the first to roll up their sleeves and get on with the job. The Virgoan social style is quiet and unassuming. A typical Virgoan will never interrupt and rarely holds the floor for more than a few minutes. They listen very carefully, however, and when they do voice an opinion, it is often startlingly intelligent. Virgoans are often very witty. They can also be brilliant mimics, due to their ability to note quietly every mannerism and characteristic of their subject.

Negative Virgoan traits include a capacity for endless worry, which can cloud their own lives unnecessarily. It also irritates more happy-go-lucky signs. Not only do Virgoans fret, they can also nag a great deal, carping relentlessly about other people's failings and sloppiness. Badly aspected Virgoans can be cold, over-analytical and obsessed with detail. They can become bogged down with trivia, delighting in what others consider boring facts. They seem obsessed with routines. Everything must always be done in the same way, and in the same order. Virgoans are great ones for inventing rules on the 'in case' principle, hedging their lives around a host of restricting rules in order to feel safe.

Career

Virgoans are the natural accountants of the zodiac, but, also being practical, calm, disciplined and cheerful, Virgoans' quiet confidence and efficiency makes them good carers. They love making a contribution, and being of service to any group. They are, however, better as members of a team than as bosses. A Virgoan in charge can easily become nit-picking and hypercritical, forever double-checking the work of others. And they can be completely intolerant of other ways of doing things.

Relationships

Though they are reliable, responsible and sensible, and can be happy in a stable relationship, Virgoans are often very difficult to live with. They find expressing emotion hard, can be tense in close relationships and are highly critical of others. They can make far better grandparents than parents. By that time of life, they may well have learned to relax and to enjoy the spontaneity of having very young children around them.

Ideal Partner

Virgoans can find most close relationships something of a trial. But if near opposites attract, they will go for deep, dark Scorpians, whose intensity adds colour to their more plodding lives, and whose sexuality can encourage them to lose their inhibitions. Gentle Pisceans, with their soft emotions, can make Virgoans realize that they can relax and enjoy home life, although both can be their own worst enemies at times. Some types of Aquarian also bring out the best in Virgo, and madcap Arians can bring a totally different energy into their lives.

COMPATIBILITY

Aries
Quick-fire Arians have a certain allure for more timid Virgoans but prove too combustible in the long term.

Cancer
Loving, sympathetic Cancerians can hit it off with sensible Virgoans, but they will cause too many scenes.

Libra
Romantic, sensitive Librans can make amenable partners for Virgoans, but they may lack staying power.

Capricorn
Virgoans appreciate the Goat's measured approach to life and love, but even they need more adventurousness.

Taurus
Both being Earth Signs, they understand each other well, but life can lack that all-important spark.

Leo
Virgoans may love to bask in reflected Leonine glory, but can find Leo's overbearing manner ultimately offputting.

Scorpio
Though attracted sexually, straightforward Virgoans are scared off by the Scorpian's sharp tongue.

Aquarius
Virgoans often admire Aquarians greatly, but their lifestyles are too divergent for lasting bonds to develop.

Gemini
They will enjoy each other's company but frivolous and flighty Geminians can frighten Virgoans away.

Virgo
Though safe, this can be a deeply dull combination. Two Virgoans will rarely have a sparkling love life.

Sagittarius
True Virgoans are often horrified by Sagittarian fecklessness and their capacity to live in the moment.

Pisces
Something about loving, needy Pisceans can bring out the best in the more supportive, well-grounded Virgoan.

LIBRA

23 September – 23 October

Sun Sign: LIBRA

Sign: THE SCALES

Ruling Planet: VENUS

Gender: MASCULINE

Element: AIR

Quality: CARDINAL

Colours: ROYAL BLUE AND PINK

Birthstone: OPAL

Compatibility: SAGITTARIUS, AQUARIUS AND TAURUS

Non-compatibility: SCORPIO, CANCER AND PISCES

The Sun In Libra

un Sign Librans make peace and harmony a priority in any situation. Normal arbiters and diplomats, they constantly seek balance, as exemplified by their sign of the Scales.

They are friendly, sunny souls whose ready smile makes them popular and trusted members of society. They are open and unsuspicious, attractive and confident. Librans are hard workers, and their search for balance enables them to play hard as well.

Librans like to be surrounded by a certain amount of order and tidiness, although they are not fanatical about it; in fact, anything overdone is alien to the Libran temperament. The axiom 'Everything in moderation' was probably invented by a Libran. Mostly Librans are cautious, preferring to weigh up their options before committing themselves to an idea or relationship. They are undemanding, often to the point of appearing to lack all ambition or drive, but how influential this trait is depends very much on their chart as a whole. True, they are usually happy to take orders and be part of a team, but they have a strong head for business, and can reveal a surprisingly steely streak. Most need the security of a regular job and a happy home, seeking always to find partners who will balance their own nature.

Librans can be unsettling: they are often inconsistent, even contradictory characters. Although they hate rudeness, they can be blunt. With such charming people as Librans, it is easy to forget what the symbolism of the Scales implies: balance is transitory, and imbalance, if only slight, is in fact

the usual state of affairs. Librans find that life is a constant effort to make
the two sides level, and make sense of its inherent duality.

CAREER

Gregarious Librans dislike working alone, but equally are not fond
of suffering under a rod of iron. They are superb at comparing and
contrasting, seeing all sides of an argument, which can make them
excellent researchers and evaluators. They enjoy working with the
public, are good listeners and can offer considered advice. Many are not
particularly ambitious on their own behalf, but are proud to be associated
with successful people and organizations.

RELATIONSHIPS

Librans see themselves as so pleasant and approachable that it comes as a
shock when friendships fail. They can be moody and liable to extreme ups
and downs, which can be very difficult to live with. Loneliness is something
a Libran finds almost impossible to endure. Always romantic, they make
romance their business, though tend to be in love with the idea of love.

IDEAL PARTNER

Romantic Librans can get along with almost anyone, from any zodiacal
sign – at least to begin with. They tend to like the enthusiasm and
unpredictability of Aquarians, while peace-loving Taureans can bring out a
Libran's more romantic streak. They are also fascinated with the glamour
and sophistication of sultry Scorpians, although they may find Scorpians'
strange moods intimidating. The more clinging Water signs, Cancerians
and Pisces, can make too many emotional demands for Librans who seek
peace and harmony.

COMPATIBILITY

Aries
They may have fun while dating but living together soon shows that self-centred Arians are too much for Librans.

Cancer
Initial attraction may not last: Librans are too uncomfortable with typical Cancerian outbursts.

Libra
Dating and sex will be fun but with two Librans together nothing will ever be settled too readily.

Capricorn
Librans' love of living it up may upset Capricornian respect for nest eggs. They have some basic differences.

Taurus
Librans can fall for beautiful and placid Taureans. This is often a lasting match made in heaven.

Leo
Librans often feel flattered by magnanimous Leonine attention, but the gloss soon wears off.

Scorpio
Straightforward Librans find Machiavellian Scorpians hard to understand but easy to fall into bed with.

Aquarius
Librans can easily become acolytes of driven Aquarians, but find them too intense for loving life partnerships.

Gemini
In many ways, Geminians and Librans are too similar, but the Twins' guiles can ultimately prove unappealing.

Virgo
Socially, these signs may hit it off, but cracks soon appear in the relationship because of Virgoan intuition.

Sagittarius
With one bound they will be free. Sagittarians offer Librans the adventure and daring that they crave.

Pisces
Truly difficult Pisceans make life hell for easy-going Librans, although they can get on well at first.

♏

SCORPIO

24 October – 22 November

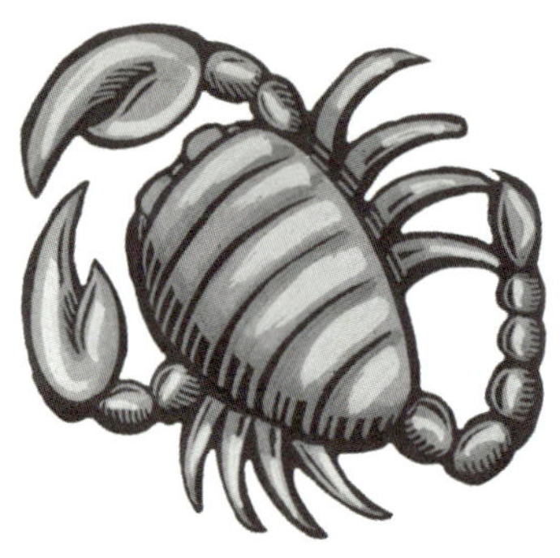

Sun Sign: Scorpio

Sign: The Scorpion

Ruling Planet: Mars and Pluto

Gender: Feminine

Element: Water

Quality: Fixed

Colours: Black and Red

Birthstone: Topaz

Compatibility: Taurus, Virgo and Libra

Non-compatibility: Aries, Leo and Sagittarius

The Sun In Scorpio

un Sign Scorpians are energetic, passionate and exciting. They are most content themselves with being forceful and fascinating, dramatically sweeping through the lives of others like mini-tornadoes. Scorpians understand the concept that death is always followed by rebirth, and they can rise like a phoenix from disastrous events in their own lives to start again with enormous, positive energy. Disappointment, bereavement, bankruptcy and illness can depress and seem, at the time, to demolish them, but not for long. Soon they are back on their feet, building new lives with genuine joy at being given the opportunity for a fresh start.

Sun Sign Scorpians have a marked tendency to jealousy and possessiveness. Profoundly secretive by nature, they often disturb others with their air of mystery, which can sometimes seem contrived. They are very theatrical and love to be outrageous.

However, there is a sting in the tail with Scorpians. The full Scorpian fury can be unsettling enough – after all, their other ruler is fiery, aggressive Mars – but to be on the receiving end of their cold, penetrating sarcasm is to be upset for days. Many Scorpians train themselves to be masters of the put-down that is devastatingly witty, but very hurtful.

These people can be wildly successful one year and bankrupt the next, although it is a process that is likely to be repeated in a curiously predictable cycle. Similarly, they can be utterly loyal and true lovers, but great passion can rapidly turn to hatred and maybe a desire for revenge.

Career

'The Devil finds work for idle hands' was never truer than in the case of an out-of-work Scorpian, whose enormous energy needs to be positively channelled, or they may turn to dubious ways of passing the time. However, once a Scorpian is fully engaged emotionally, there are few more ambitious workers. Not surprisingly, Scorpians can be rather disruptive in the workplace. They see everything – status, pay and perks – as a reflection of their own worth, and can make formidable rivals. Many Scorpians find life easier when self-employed, although they do like to have regular contact with others.

Relationships

Intense and sexual, Scorpians are not easy to live with. They are not above using sex as a form of control, although they don't indulge in emotional blackmail as much as Cancerians. Many Scorpians are much more interested in the image of sexual conquests than in the act itself. Scorpians can be very vindictive and vengeful. Never expect to walk away from a romance with a Scorpian unscathed. They make demanding parents and can put too much pressure on their children.

Ideal Partner

Scorpians, with their love of drama, may often be attracted to their own sign for that reason alone. It seldom works out, however, because of a Scorpian's temperamental nature. Underneath a Scorpian's theatrical exterior is someone who just wants to be loved. Their polar sign of Taurus can give them the emotional security that they crave. Virgoans, too, share the ability to calm Scorpians. Well-balanced Librans also share the capacity to humour Scorpians and see the needy person inside.

COMPATIBILITY

Aries
Arians may bring a breath of fresh air into the claustrophobic world of the Scorpian, but they can be too demanding.

Cancer
Devoted Cancerians are too normal for quirky Scorpians, and their emotional highs and lows get short shrift.

Libra
Scorpians often fascinate Librans and they can enjoy very passionate sex but Scorpians are just too dark.

Capricorn
Capricornian repression has little appeal for sexually adventurous Scorpians and may lead to frostiness.

Taurus
Perhaps curiously, Scorpio's opposite sign can prove very appealing and make a long-term relationship work well.

Leo
Relationships will be passionate and sex exciting but Scorpians do not take kindly to Leonine attempts to dominate.

Scorpio
Fellow Scorpians often get on well, having the same unusual interests, but may fall out of love too easily.

Aquarius
Scorpians often respect the causes espoused by Aquarians but can find them too involved in 'boring' politics.

Gemini
Flighty, wily Geminians can charm Scorpians – but not for long. In the end, they're just too shallow for Scorpio.

Virgo
The more sociable Virgoans can be complementary partners but not if they embody Virgoan obsessive tidiness.

Sagittarius
Scorpians find these wild children very charming but do not go for the insecurity or lack of permanent lifestyle.

Pisces
Both signs are complex and intense with extreme demands. Lasting and loving relationships are unlikely.

SAGITTARIUS

23 November – 21 December

Sun Sign: SAGITTARIUS

Sign: THE ARCHER OR CENTAUR

Ruling Planet: JUPITER

Gender: MASCULINE

Element: FIRE

Quality: MUTABLE

Colours: DARK BLUE AND PURPLE

Birthstone: TURQUOISE

Compatibility: AQUARIUS AND LIBRA

Non-compatibility: CANCER, SCORPIO AND TAURUS

The Sun In Sagittarius

un Sign Sagittarians are some of the most likeable folk around: open, optimistic, enthusiastic and tolerant. Their ruler Jupiter is traditionally supposed to be lucky, and this largest of all the planets in the solar system does seem to bestow very positive opportunities on Sagittarians. Possibly this is because their attitude actively invites such opportunity. Exuberant, Sagittarians are adept at inspiring and encouraging more pessimistic and cautious souls, although they can be appallingly foolhardy, getting themselves into some worrying situations.

Many people born under the sign of the Archer find it hard to concentrate for very long on any one subject unless it captures their imagination, and then they can give their whole selves to it for hours. Their keen, restless minds are always looking to the future, trying to be one jump ahead – and often succeeding in being at least two. The joyful Sagittarians have an infectious curiosity, and are an interesting blend of the studious and the very physical, for they are essentially outdoor types.

Sagittarians are also inclined to philosophy and religion, although they rarely become fanatics. They love discussing their ideas, often late into the night, and are happy to share their home with a large number of very diverse people.

However, excessive Sagittarian energy can be disconcerting. People born under this sign tend to flit from job to job, lover to lover and home to home. Some may never settle, remaining life's gypsies. Other people may find this restlessness disturbing, especially the more security-minded materialists, such as Taurus or Virgo, whose home is their castle.

CAREER

Sagittarians pursue anything that gives free rein to their adventurous spirits. They will never persist with any job that limits them. Making money is usually of secondary importance to them. They are not seriously materialistic; on the whole their working lives are focused on deeper matters. Many Sagittarians lack staying power. They have wonderfully inspired ideas that they fully intend to turn into a concrete result, but in a very short space of time they forget all about it, become disillusioned, and turn their attention to the next tempting project.

RELATIONSHIPS

Since Sagittarius is a Fire Sign, people born under it are highly sexed, and have no time for prudish attitudes. However, they can be considerably less keen on settling down with one partner. Some never decide, and go blowing through life solo, always surrounded by a circle of admirers. As free spirits, Sagittarians need understanding partners who can cope with abrupt changes of plan. Any disharmony distresses them, and often the only way they can cope with it is by running away.

IDEAL PARTNER

Most Sagittarians prefer to have a range of partners, chosen from all signs of the zodiac, but when they do settle down, they need to spend their lives with easy-going, tolerant but organized people who make few demands and who are not particularly jealous or possessive. This is something of a tall order, but certain Aquarians and Librans fit the bill. Those who are definitely not compatible with Sagittarians are clinging Cancerians, intense Scorpians and jealous Taureans.

COMPATIBILITY

Aries
Aries will usually try to dominate fellow Fire Sign Sagittarius – which will only drive them further away.

Cancer
The famous Cancerian compassion and talent for homemaking is wasted on these free spirits.

Libra
Librans and Sagittarians are a good match, inspiring and supporting each other. Physically very compatible.

Capricorn
Sagittarians find Goats hard to understand. Their caution is anathema to the untamed Sagittarian spirit.

Taurus
Tame, conventional Taureans often prove too stodgy for idiosyncratic and sometimes eccentric Sagittarians.

Leo
The Leonine energy and verve is attractive to fiery Sagittarius, but sooner or later they will clash.

Scorpio
Dark Scorpians often try to ensnare charming Sagittarians, but intense physicality doesn't mean enduring love.

Aquarius
This can be the perfect match. Both signs have little regard for the establishment or convention.

Gemini
Superficially on the same wavelength, but Geminians play too many games for innocent Sagittarians.

Virgo
Steady, organized and repressed, Virgoans are the complete opposite of unrealistic Sagittarians.

Sagittarius
Fellow Sagittarians will get on well and fuel each other's madcap schemes. Romantic, yes. Practical, no.

Pisces
Sagittarians have little time for self-indulgent scenes, so touchy Pisceans are unlikely to make good life partners.

CAPRICORN

22 December – 20 January

Sun Sign: Capricorn

Sign: The Goat

Ruling Planet: Saturn

Gender: Feminine

Element: Earth

Quality: Cardinal

Colours: Dark Brown, Black, Grey

Birthstone: Garnet

Compatibility: Taurus and Virgo

Non-compatibility: Sagittarius and Aries

The Sun In Capricorn

Sun Sign Capricornians are disciplined, sensible and sensitive. If that makes them sound excessively cold and dull, they can be, but often they show remarkable ambition, kindness and gentle, often self-deprecating, humour. Traditionally, their ruling planet Saturn is concerned with the tough lessons of life: illness, restriction, old age and death, but modern astrologers realize that this picture is far too gloomy. While Saturn can be a tough teacher, often repeatedly putting Capricornians through a steep learning curve, it can also galvanize them into action.

Capricornians tend to be cautious by nature, sensing pitfalls and obstacles and standing back from problems. This can make them pessimistic and disinclined to move forward. However, the whole point of the Saturnine influence is to present them with a series of challenges that will never be too difficult for them to overcome. Once Capricornians have come to understand the true nature of their path, it will be easier for them to rise above the mundane pettiness and worries that often beset them.

Sticklers for detail, and methodical to a fault, Capricornians are superb organizers, happy to deal with paperwork and the daily business of life. They are not natural stars like Leos or Scorpians, but usually seek to oil the wheels behind the scenes and make everything run smoothly. They can seem joyless and obsessed with doing the right thing, but when they let go and relax they are charming, delightful companions, with a wonderfully dry sense of humour.

Career

Sun Sign Capricornians are industrious and formidably organized, so they make superb administrators. They frequently have their eye on the top job, and are content to work their way towards it in gradual stages. Dutiful, rather austere and unimaginative, they are very good with money matters and scrupulously honest, which makes them ideal in positions of trust. They tend to have very low self-worth, and see their work as a reflection of the respect that they have earned.

Relationships

Capricornians can be surprisingly passionate behind closed doors – after all, theirs is the sign of the Goat! However, they take a while to warm up.

Capricornians are seldom easy-going and can, in fact, be rather dour. They need to be encouraged to lighten up. They can be over-keen on pouring cold water on the bright ideas of more enthusiastic family members. Some Capricornians are constantly worried about money. To them, destitution is only around the corner.

Ideal Partner

Capricornians need a strong, loving partner who neither whines nor clings. Dreamy Pisceans rarely fit the bill, and fellow Water Sign Cancerians are usually far too demanding. Earthy Taureans and Virgoans, who have a similar fondness for order, but possess added charm, possibly make the best partners for the wintry Capricornians. It would be a mistake for a typical Goat even to consider a relationship with a happy-go-lucky Sagittarian or a wild-child Arian.

COMPATIBILITY

Aries
Fiery, tempestuous Arians may be appealingly different, but this opposite sign will be too cold to attract for long.

Cancer
Cancerian emotion can drive Capricornians mad, although their compassion and loving home have certain attractions.

Libra
Librans' love of the social whirl can cause problems for the more withdrawn and hesitant type of Capricornian.

Capricorn
Two wintry Goats together may not make for much empathizing but sometimes like works with like.

Taurus
Earthy and controlled Taureans have a lot to offer the Goat, and they can bring out the passion in each other.

Leo
Capricornians admire Leonine style and dash, but are fearful of such high-profile egocentrics.

Scorpio
Intrigued by fascinating Scorpio, Capricorn may make a serious error of judgement – and live to regret it.

Aquarius
This combination can work, if only because Aquarians can get on with most people if they are prepared to compromise.

Gemini
Gregarious, persuasive Geminians can charm reserved Capricornians, but the Goat remains distrustful.

Virgo
Calm, self-contained Virgoans often make excellent partners for cautious, conventional Capricornians.

Sagittarius
Unfettered by practicalities, Sagittarians seriously upset Capricornian respect for the more traditional way of life.

Pisces
Contradictory and often unhappy Pisceans will bewilder Capricornians, who are scared by overt emotion.

AQUARIUS

21 January – 18 February

Sun Sign: AQUARIUS

Sign: THE WATER CARRIER

Ruling Planet: URANUS AND SATURN

Gender: MASCULINE

Element: AIR

Quality: FIXED

Colour: ALL THE COLOURS OF THE RAINBOW

Birthstone: AMETHYST

Compatibility: PISCES AND CAPRICORN

Non-compatibility: ALMOST NO ONE – AT LEAST IN THEORY

The Sun In Aquarius

Sun Sign Aquarians are friendly, idealistic, independent and humanitarian. That said, they are also the most varied set of individuals within one zodiacal group, so it is difficult to make generalizations about them. However, what is certain is that they tend to be extremely capable, kind, charitable and very forward-looking.

Aquarians are always eager to improve themselves and the world around them, and are well aware of the spiritual side to life. They frequently hold strong political views, and often mount campaigns against some form of injustice. Brave, free-spirited Aquarians are always true friends to the downtrodden, but find it hard to translate all that 'love and light' into close relationships. They are often bad at creating a loving environment for themselves. For them, charity rarely begins at home.

Aquarius is an Air Sign, and those born under this sign need their personal space, both literally and figuratively. They hate limits and react very badly to being told what to do, although they can often be surprisingly dictatorial themselves. They are independent and logical and their real talents frequently belie their rather unworldly image.

Despite their rather airy-fairy image, Aquarians are surprisingly adept with technology, realizing that it is the way forward. This is the key to their thinking. They rarely look back and believe that the future is all-important. Their brave new world will be caring, compassionate and informed, and they are willing to work hard to ensure that it comes about.

CAREER

Aquarians can turn their hands very successfully to most things, since they are very determined individuals. Most are hardworking, perhaps even driven, in their chosen field. They are best at work that involves them in improving the lot of humanity in some way. They see life as a series of golden opportunities, and if money happens to come their way, so much the better. They are natural problem-solvers, with a practical streak and marked ability to think laterally.

RELATIONSHIPS

Aquarians are not good at close relationships, despite all their caring-and-sharing attitudes. They tend to be very wary of emotion, often misconstruing it as mere sentiment that makes irritating demands on their affections. In their minds, they belong to the world, not to one partner or family. They need tolerance for their peculiarities, and a large measure of independence, so much so that many Aquarians choose to remain unattached. In many respects, they are happier with friends and co-crusaders than with life-partners.

IDEAL PARTNER

Anyone who is also an idealistic free spirit will be suitable for an Aquarian. They detest emotional blackmail so clingers such as the more badly aspected Cancerian need not apply. Sometimes they respond well to Pisceans, and the same applies to well-grounded Capricornians. In general, though, Aquarians are so individualistic that they could settle down with almost anyone. However, the same may not be true of the other half of the relationship.

COMPATIBILITY

Aries
These two signs share world-saving ambitions and can have powerful sexual magnetism, but it may not last long.

Cancer
Cancerians can provide emotional support as long as they are not too clingy or emotional.

Libra
Librans may fall under the Aquarian spell, but it may be hero-worship rather than love that fuels the relationship.

Capricorn
Oddly staid and cautious Capricornians can succeed in winning the love and protection of Aquarians.

Taurus
Taureans are disconcerted by Aquarian conventionality and rebellion, and will usually steer clear of it.

Leo
Leonine nobility may be appealing but their grandness cuts no ice with egalitarian Aquarians.

Scorpio
Scorpians' interest in deep, mystical subjects appeals to New Age Aquarians, but can be too dark for peace-lovers.

Aquarius
Two world-changing humanitarians must get on – or are their egos too demanding for such a union to work?

Gemini
Aquarians understand the Geminian restlessness and drive, but add their own, more profound, idealism.

Virgo
Aquarians may mock safe, steady Virgoans' obsession with analysis and order as being too retentive.

Sagittarius
These two signs are similarly rebellious and free-spirited, but Sagittarian indiscipline may threaten the grand plan.

Pisces
Dreamy, otherworldly Pisceans can find lasting love with mystical Aquarians, who will overlook their intensity.

PISCES

19 February – 20 March

Sun Sign: PISCES

Sign: TWO FISH

Ruling Planet: NEPTUNE AND JUPITER

Gender: FEMININE

Element: WATER

Quality: MUTABLE

Colours: SEA GREEN AND MAUVE

Birthstone: AQUAMARINE

Compatibility: AQUARIUS, PISCES AND VIRGO

Non-compatibility: CANCER, SCORPIO AND CAPRICORN

The Sun In Pisces

Sun Sign Pisceans are emotional, dreamy, insecure people with strong creative instincts. Poetic and intuitive, they often seem out of place in the everyday world. All the same, many Pisceans achieve great things. They are kind, sensitive souls, who delight in the happiness and fulfilment of others. Sometimes they go too far in this regard, for they can live their entire lives in the shadow of more ambitious people, and never achieve their own potential. Born under an archetypically Feminine Water Sign, Pisceans seek above all to establish peace, harmony and love.

Pisceans tend to view life through rose-tinted spectacles. In some cases, this is all that gets them through, because a negative side of this sign is the ease with which Pisceans can be cast down. Once this happens, all motivation is gone and Pisceans become moody. Many will do anything rather than face cold, stark reality, finding refuge in escapism of one sort or another.

Like their sign – two fish swimming in opposite directions – Pisceans have an indecisive streak. They may be afraid of offering their own opinions, although at the same time they resent it when others take command.

Pisceans are secretive, and can be deceitful. They may lack the depth and scope of black Scorpionic vengeance, but they can still be nasty. Of course, many are delightful, open people but there is almost always an underlying feeling of not belonging, of lacking a voice, of being faceless, which manifests as resentment at the assertiveness of other people.

Career

Pisceans are almost always in touch with their unconscious minds, and once they learn to deal with this effectively, they can become very successful in creative fields. They are not natural organizers. Often, they do not seek promotion, but are more content to take a back seat and get on with their job. They are very good team members. Piscean restlessness is often assuaged by having more than one job, or by pursuing a hobby very seriously.

Relationships

Many Pisceans can be very loving partners for life, although they are too restless to settle without the occasional change of scene. They can usually recognize the weaknesses of others, and, if cornered, can go for them vindictively. They also do a very effective line in huge emotional scenes, although these tend to be over almost as soon as they have begun. Even so, many Pisceans are truly charming, hospitable folk, justly proud of their homemaking. Romantic, they can easily fall for rogues.

Ideal Partner

Aquarians tend to bond romantically with Pisces, although they will not easily endure too many emotional outbursts or any vindictiveness. However, the organizational abilities of Aquarians often complement Piscean dreaminess very well. Two Pisceans together will never get anything done, although their dreams may be truly exciting. Earthy Virgoans can often find happiness with Pisceans, and even, in some cases, lordly Leos will magnanimously allow Pisces to live in their shadow, which may well suit both of them.

COMPATIBILITY

Aries
Domineering and inflexible Arians find oddball and effusive Pisceans too difficult to live with.

Cancer
At worst, weepy, over-the-top Cancerians and moody Pisceans make for a nightmare domestic scenario.

Libra
The last thing peace-seeking Librans need is Piscean 'baggage' and moodiness. This relationship won't last.

Capricorn
Unemotional Goats find Piscean excesses beyond belief, and won't even begin to woo them.

Taurus
Pisceans' innate moodiness and contrariness can seriously annoy equable, well-grounded Taureans.

Leo
Lordly Leos are very sexy and charming, but touchy Pisceans will soon back away from all that ambition.

Scorpio
While these two signs can easily fall for each other, they are far too difficult to make the necessary compromises.

Aquarius
These two signs are soul mates and made for each other. Aquarian loftiness can easily overlook Piscean angst.

Gemini
There may be a strong initial attraction between these two signs, but party animal Geminians can seem too light.

Virgo
Pisceans can easily come to love Virgoans' charm and sense of order. This can be a lasting romance.

Sagittarius
Demanding Pisceans will be hurt and puzzled by the Sagittarian tendency to disappear without a word.

Pisces
A winning combination – the organizational skills of one complementing the dreaminess of the other.

MOON SIGNS

Moon Signs

So far, we have seen how the Sun influences our outward manner, our major personality traits, our career disposition, relationships and love life. The Moon, on the other hand, as the second most important body in our solar system, influences our emotions, our inner life and our inherited traits and characteristics.

Where Sun Signs span a 28-day period, following the path of the Earth's rotation around the Sun throughout the course of the year, your Moon Sign covers just over two days, as the Moon takes just a month to visit all the signs of the Zodiac, spending about two full days in each sign, before its cycle begins again.

This section of the book provides a summary of the major characteristics of each combination of Sun and Moon Signs – for example, the personality of someone whose Sun Sign is Taurus and Moon Sign is Aries – followed by full entries devoted to each Moon placement.

DETERMINING YOUR MOON SIGN

To determine your Moon Sign, you will need to know your time of birth (the more precise the better), along with the time zone you were born in and, of course, your date of birth. With this information, use an online astrology calculator (such as www.astrocal.co.uk/moon-sign-calculator) to find out what your Moon sign is. Then, refer to the Sun and Moon Sign Combinations on the following pages, along with the relevant entry to your Moon Sign, to gain a deeper understanding of your true character as influenced by the power of the Moon.

Sun and Moon Sign Combinations

SUN ARIES, MOON ARIES: Enthusiastic, motivated and quick-witted. Egocentric and impatient. They always aim for the top, seeking the glittering prizes. They can be ruthless.

SUN ARIES, MOON TAURUS: Artistic, sensuous and down to earth. Stubborn and dogmatic. They love tradition but can be fearful of change – even if it's for the better.

SUN ARIES, MOON GEMINI: Bright, articulate, persuasive. Overly sharp-tongued and lacking in stamina. Excellent media people, but have erratic energy flow, so need to pace themselves.

SUN ARIES, MOON CANCER: Business-like, genial and determined. Tough façade hides vulnerability. They carry very old emotional scars and need to open up to a soul mate.

SUN ARIES, MOON LEO: Extrovert, high flyer – the natural stars of the zodiac. Insensitive to others, misses finer points. Often a huge success – thanks to the hard work and loyalty of others.

SUN ARIES, MOON VIRGO: Efficient, logical and analytical. Over-critical and fussy. Can harbour wild fantasies and surprising ambitions – which they should encourage from time to time.

SUN ARIES, MOON LIBRA: Ambitious, balanced, passionate and caring. May be over-optimistic and gullible, but their divine innocence can protect them against many unpleasant situations and people.

SUN ARIES, MOON SCORPIO: Intense, focused and motivated. Can be intimidating and too theatrical. Lots of energy and commitment, but take disappointment very hard. Even so, they bounce back.

SUN ARIES, MOON SAGITTARIUS: Motivating, encouraging, restless and daring. Insensitive and blunt. Something of the eternal child – complete with foot-stomping tantrums.

SUN ARIES, MOON CAPRICORN: Ambitious, determined and tough. Domineering and cold, but has a surprising capacity to hero-worship others – from a safe distance and secretly.

SUN ARIES, MOON AQUARIUS: Idealistic and humanitarian. Tactless and outspoken. Vast resources of energy and resilience and many – often conflicting – goals.

SUN ARIES, MOON PISCES: Confident exterior hides timid interior. Can be something of a zealot. Seeks to wear different masks for different occasions in order to impress.

SUN TAURUS, MOON ARIES: Poised exterior hides raging inner ambition. Opinionated and dogmatic. Can feel hard done by and demand apologies where none are required, but often back down if stood up to.

SUN TAURUS, MOON TAURUS: Faithful, musical and creative. Stubborn and temperamental. Committed to maintaining old-fashioned values.

SUN TAURUS, MOON GEMINI: Articulate, witty and excitable, with good ideas. Lack stamina. Respects and admires people with organizational skills, and those who are good with money.

SUN TAURUS, MOON CANCER: Caring, home-loving and encouraging. Less secure about own ambitions and may lack drive, but excellent at supporting others and helping them to achieve their dreams.

SUN TAURUS, MOON LEO: Loyal and colourful, dramatic and deliberate. Inflexible and opinionated. Good organizers and natural leaders, although may be inclined to laziness.

SUN TAURUS, MOON VIRGO: Meticulous, orderly and organized. Family-loving, articulate and musical. Hypercritical and often rather dull. Tend to have a hidden poetic streak, and can be surprisingly passionate lovers.

SUN TAURUS, MOON LIBRA: Caring, compassionate and loving. Can be ambitious. Lazy and erratic, but the heart is in the right place. They seek above all to be peace-makers.

SUN TAURUS, MOON SCORPIO: Independent, strong and artistic. Inclined to take too much on. Obstinate and inclined to bottle up old regrets and disappointments. Need to open their hearts more to confidants.

SUN TAURUS, MOON SAGITTARIUS: Pious, studious, academic. Intrigued by the idea of adventure. Tend to be lazy, judgemental and dogmatic, but can indulge in flights of fancy and become rather unrealistic.

SUN TAURUS, MOON CAPRICORN: Adept in business, sensible and shrewd. Insecure in personal relationships, but secret romantics at heart. They have a desperate need to be loved and understood.

SUN TAURUS, MOON AQUARIUS: Confident, bright, free thinking, gregarious. Can lay down the law but essentially they are fairly happy-go-lucky and tolerant. Rarely nostalgic – very forward-looking.

SUN TAURUS, MOON PISCES: Determined and creative, compassionate and caring. Can be gullible and naive but many see this as rather charming. They have an arty side to their personality.

SUN GEMINI, MOON ARIES: Interesting, innovative thinkers and excellent in the media. Superficial and sometimes cruel, although they may not realize how much they hurt others.

SUN GEMINI, MOON TAURUS: Patient, intelligent and persistent. Morose and emotionally insecure. Can have bursts of energy and inspiration, which quickly die down again.

SUN GEMINI, MOON GEMINI: Extremely quick-witted and amusing. Tense, glib and lacking in stamina. Can feel very isolated and lonely – even in a large crowd.

SUN GEMINI, MOON CANCER: Communicative, open and home-loving. Weak-willed and possessive – easy to influence. Can become a doormat, although rebelliousness is not unknown.

SUN GEMINI, MOON LEO: Enthusiastic, attractive and creative. Childish and egocentric. Can be very opinionated but can easily be charmed out of any inflexibility. Moody and erratic.

SUN GEMINI, MOON VIRGO: Adaptable, lateral thinker and rather intellectual. Nervy, lacking in ambition but tend to admire others who aim for the top.

SUN GEMINI, MOON LIBRA: Flirtatious, sociable and flighty. Pompous and self-congratulatory. Feel threatened by those with strong beliefs or opinions. Need to be centred and calm.

SUN GEMINI, MOON SCORPIO: Deep, possessor of dark secrets and often fascinating. Perverse, vulnerable and lonely. Love to explore the mysterious side of life. Can become hooked on the paranormal.

SUN GEMINI, MOON SAGITTARIUS: Studious, physical and adventurous. Insensitive and outspoken. Can be unrealistic and naive. Need to plan for the future.

SUN GEMINI, MOON CAPRICORN: Good with words, intelligent. Emotionally uncommunicative and cold but they often cry inside. Often lonely and lost – need a soul mate.

SUN GEMINI, MOON AQUARIUS: Clever and bright, instinctively knowing. Wary of expressing emotions or becoming too deeply involved romantically and sexually. May avoid commitment.

SUN GEMINI, MOON PISCES: Extrovert, fun and very communicative. Inwardly tense and insecure, and in need of romance and sensuality. Intuitive, moody and often somewhat psychic.

SUN CANCER, MOON ARIES: Understanding, business-like and caring. Over-competitive and restless. Can easily become intense about all relationships, both business and personal. They need emotional commitment.

SUN CANCER, MOON TAURUS: Compassionate, sensual and family-centred, but with a tendency to be rather lazy, sulky and moody. Often need cheering up by friends on fun nights out.

SUN CANCER, MOON GEMINI: Genial, ambitious and quick-witted. Guileful and manipulative, often great plotters and particularly good at revenge.

SUN CANCER, MOON CANCER: Kind, sensitive, upholders of traditional values. Live in the past, are over-emotional and possessive. Can become hysterical if crossed. Have a tendency to cut their nose off to spite their face.

SUN CANCER, MOON LEO: Great integrity, passionate and loving. Dogmatic and insecure, but basically kind and compassionate. Above all – need to be understood.

SUN CANCER, MOON VIRGO: Good with illness. Business-like, hardworking, with good – almost total – recall. Excessive worriers, mean-minded and penny-pinching, although secretly longing to be wildly extravagant.

SUN CANCER, MOON LIBRA: Ambitious, family-centred and peace-loving. Unrealistic, with little grasp of detail but can be good at seeing the overall picture. Often very charming and urbane.

SUN CANCER, MOON SCORPIO: Always after the centre stage. Very intense and sometimes psychic. Can suffer from depression and be rather secretive. Great capacity for passionate love.

SUN CANCER, MOON SAGITTARIUS: Family-loving, free-spirited and joyful. Over-optimistic, unrealistic and inclined to daydream. Often charming but feckless. Need to be somewhat more organized.

SUN CANCER, MOON CAPRICORN: Perceptive in business, ambitious and hardworking. Parsimonious and pessimistic, often seeing life in joyless terms. Can have intense, but secret, passions.

SUN CANCER, MOON AQUARIUS: Communicative, articulate and adroit. Manipulative and self-centred but can work hard for the common good. A good grasp of the long term.

SUN CANCER, MOON PISCES: Psychic, sensitive and compassionate, and a fierce champion of the underdog. Moody and fearful, and inclined to suffer from nightmares. Loving but emotionally very needy.

SUN LEO, MOON ARIES: Encouraging, enthusiastic and courageous. Domineering and callous, and given to wild tantrums if crossed. However, likely to forgive and forget fairly easily.

SUN LEO, MOON TAURUS: Traditional, placid and dependable. Can sometimes appear boring and stubborn but can occasionally surprise people by being the life and soul of the party.

SUN LEO, MOON GEMINI: Quick-witted, innovative thinkers – natural leaders. Although inclined to be sharp-tongued and insensitive, and capable of lashing out without thinking, they are basically kind and well-meaning.

SUN LEO, MOON CANCER: Protective, nurturing and comforting. Over-possessive and hysterical, yet often puzzled and frightened by the emotional needs of others.

SUN LEO, MOON LEO: Successful, individual and a natural star. Domineering and unrealistic, and can ruthlessly exploit others. Charming and inspiring.

SUN LEO, MOON VIRGO: Logical, methodical, kind and decent. Sometimes petty-minded and abrupt, although this cool exterior hides a genuinely compassionate heart.

SUN LEO, MOON LIBRA: Stylish, flirtatious and successful. Egocentric with a tendency to be promiscuous and to abuse the trust of others. Surprisingly bold in coming to the rescue. Something of a hero.

SUN LEO, MOON SCORPIO: Hard-working, theatrical, colourful and witty. Melodramatic and intimidating, with a tendency to ride roughshod over the sensibilities of others. Embarrassed and contrite when this is pointed out.

SUN LEO, MOON SAGITTARIUS: Warm-hearted, enthusiastic and adventurous. Impatient, restless, too independent. Great explorers and pioneers. Able to tolerate physical discomfort and help others less fortunate than themselves.

SUN LEO, MOON CAPRICORN: Efficient, traditional and ambitious. Insecure underneath with a great need for demonstrations of affection. Can find it hard to express emotional commitment.

SUN LEO, MOON AQUARIUS: Faithful, honest, fair and idealistic. Opinionated and dogmatic. Need several different outlets for philanthropic urges. Busy and committed.

SUN LEO, MOON PISCES: Kind-hearted, psychic and caring. Easily distressed or distracted but quick to help others. Can become over-demanding in close relationships.

SUN VIRGO, MOON ARIES: Clever, versatile, adaptable and good with words. Sarcastic and hurtful but not without some grace and gentleness. Can be very amusing.

SUN VIRGO, MOON TAURUS: Solid, reliable, helpful and good with their hands. Not innovative or original thinkers, but immensely admiring of those who are. Very good supporter of family and friends.

SUN VIRGO, MOON GEMINI: Quick to speak and act, and good at research. Frightened of strong emotion and something of a cold fish outwardly, but secretly desperate to find love.

SUN VIRGO, MOON CANCER: Clever, shrewd, family-loving. Excessive worriers and very possessive. Can be hoarders, being totally convinced that civilization as we know it is about to collapse. Fond of conspiracy theories.

SUN VIRGO, MOON LEO: Honest, enthusiastic and meticulous. Insecure and sometimes unambitious, although they make efforts from time to time to better themselves. Reserved but deep.

SUN VIRGO, MOON VIRGO: Kind, reliable and organized. Petty-minded and can be pennypinching. Terrible worriers. Good at analysis, investigation and research. Can seem over-intellectual and intimidating.

SUN VIRGO, MOON LIBRA: Diplomatic, organized and good team workers. Indecisive and hesitant but excellent at seeing all round a problem. Sociable and charming.

SUN VIRGO, MOON SCORPIO: Intense, incisive and profound thinkers. Outwardly unemotional and uncommunicative but a seething mass of hidden feelings. Often harbour lifelong – and sometimes unrequited – passions.

SUN VIRGO, MOON SAGITTARIUS: Open, amenable, gregarious and studious. Impatient and slapdash, over-eager to move on to the next project. Can be impractical and unworldly.

SUN VIRGO, MOON CAPRICORN: Serious, business-like and meticulous. Self-centred, cold and lacking spontaneity. Need to lighten up and have fun. Emotional commitment is difficult.

SUN VIRGO, MOON AQUARIUS: Independent, philosophical and studious. Insensitive to the emotional needs of others but determined to live their lives for them, whether they like it or not.

SUN VIRGO, MOON PISCES: Deep, psychic, intuitive and caring to the point of martyrdom. Doormat mentality and over-possessive, but can be very kind and understanding and extremely supportive of others.

SUN LIBRA, MOON ARIES: Excellent in emergencies, pioneering and adventurous. Lack stamina, can be self-centred and unreliable on a day-to-day basis. Often attractive and charming.

SUN LIBRA, MOON TAURUS: Creative and artistic, musical, stylish and practical. Can be lazy and erratic, but once motivated can work hard and become successful. Good homemakers.

SUN LIBRA, MOON GEMINI: Good technical mind, quick, intelligent, practical and innovative. Over-dependent on others. Glib and often speak without thinking, tearing through life in a tremendous hurry, rarely finishing anything.

SUN LIBRA, MOON CANCER: Amiable, caring, home loving and efficient. Too selfless and over-altruistic – and easily walked over by others. Can be naive, but this innocence is very attractive.

SUN LIBRA, MOON LEO: Quick, clever and sharp-tongued. Incurably romantic and melodramatic. Love to make a splash. Can be over-extravagant and feckless. Great fun to be with.

SUN LIBRA, MOON VIRGO: Meticulous, versatile, genial and good with words. Can lack confidence and ambition but can be motivated to achieve great things.

SUN LIBRA, MOON LIBRA: Charming, stylish and gregarious. Can be slothful and unfocused, although they can certainly move very fast when chasing the object of their passion.

SUN LIBRA, MOON SCORPIO: Forceful, magnetic and sexual. Can be dominating, power-mad and 'over-the-top' but given to retreating into solitude from time to time to recharge their batteries.

SUN LIBRA, MOON SAGITTARIUS: Good with detail and logical argument. Fair and just but with a restless spirit that needs many changes of direction. Can ignore the emotional needs of others.

SUN LIBRA, MOON CAPRICORN: Tough negotiator, dedicated worker, shrewd and perceptive. Cynical and sceptical but can be a pushover in love. A great capacity for passion.

SUN LIBRA, MOON AQUARIUS: Quick-witted, intelligent and strong. A good leader. Can be interfering and arrogant with no time for the niceties of others' feelings. Good at planning.

SUN LIBRA, MOON PISCES: Intuitive, romantic and creative. Lacking in concentration and inclined to daydream. Apparently spontaneous and childlike, which many find attractive, although there is a manipulative side.

SUN SCORPIO, MOON ARIES: Intense and brave. Good leaders. Confrontational, aggressive and over-dramatic with a strong sense of destiny that drives them to become very successful.

SUN SCORPIO, MOON TAURUS: Dependable, erotic and musical. Stubborn, stolid and sometimes a little dull. However, they can be passionate and occasionally have exotic interests.

SUN SCORPIO, MOON GEMINI: Quick-witted, intuitive and a good judge of people. Cynical and world-weary, but still determined to enjoy life. Sometimes love crowds; at other times seek solitude.

SUN SCORPIO, MOON CANCER: Intuitive, magnetic and caring. Moody, suspicious – and frightened – of intimacy. Not an easy type, but once won over tends to become a lifelong friend.

SUN SCORPIO, MOON LEO: Persistent and faithful with great powers of endurance. Inflexible, dogmatic and can be hurtful. Set high standards for themselves and others.

SUN SCORPIO, MOON VIRGO: Meticulous, intelligent and dedicated. Suspicious of emotion and close relationships, but once in love it is usually for ever.

SUN SCORPIO, MOON LIBRA: Purposeful, diplomatic, career-minded and good at mediation. Uncomfortable with close family ties, often preferring to live apart from relatives. Too independent.

SUN SCORPIO, MOON SCORPIO: Passionate, dramatic, assertive and often highly motivated and successful. Intimidating and intense but can translate this intensity into extreme loyalty, either to an individual or a belief system.

SUN SCORPIO, MOON SAGITTARIUS: Funny, persistent, well grounded and good at research. Can be erratic and have unrealistic moods. Need to find a sensible pace to maintain workable energy levels.

SUN SCORPIO, MOON CAPRICORN: Serious, ambitious and determined. Lacking spontaneity and a sense of fun but often long desperately to do something surprising. Secretly seek a true soul mate.

SUN SCORPIO, MOON AQUARIUS: Determined, focused and ambitious. Dogmatic and arrogant – benevolent dictator type. Not swayed by flattery or romance, but quietly appreciative of both from time to time.

SUN SCORPIO, MOON PISCES: Altruistic, caring and artistic. Can be sarcastic and occasionally vindictive – especially if crossed in love, when they can avenge themselves with great imagination.

SUN SAGITTARIUS, MOON ARIES: Pioneering, restless and innovative. Impatient and impulsive, and bad with lasting intimacy, although relationships are often passionate while they last.

SUN SAGITTARIUS, MOON TAURUS: Imaginative, practical, motivating and artistic. Inclined to be self-indulgent, lazy and undisciplined but can pull themselves together when necessary, often producing some very successful work.

SUN SAGITTARIUS, MOON GEMINI: Good with words, pro-active and motivated. Impatient – lacking stamina and persistence. Excellent at inspiring others. Good delegators.

SUN SAGITTARIUS, MOON CANCER: Artistic, psychic, intuitive and caring. Can be deluded and unrealistic, with little grasp of day-to-day practicalities. Great daydreamers.

SUN SAGITTARIUS, MOON LEO: Entertaining and extrovert, amusing and gregarious. Often selfish and demanding, especially with their nearest and dearest.

SUN SAGITTARIUS, MOON VIRGO: Organized, thorough and often profound. Dogmatic and pompous, though somewhat afraid of strong emotion, finding heart-to-hearts threatening. Tend to hide behind a mask.

SUN SAGITTARIUS, MOON LIBRA: Forceful, persuasive and analytical. Tend to be fashionable, attractive and stylish – but can be a little impatient and arrogant. Sometimes tetchy.

SUN SAGITTARIUS, MOON SCORPIO: An efficient and sometimes inspired mind. Incisive, dogged and profound. Good at lateral thinking. Can be intolerant and peevish.

SUN SAGITTARIUS, MOON SAGITTARIUS: Free-spirited, independent, pioneering and energetic. Impatient with other lifestyles and quick to criticize, but find it easy to forgive and forget.

SUN SAGITTARIUS, MOON CAPRICORN: Bright, persistent and amusing company, with great ambitions. Afraid of emotion and too ready to condemn, with a tendency to pessimism and lack of self-esteem.

SUN SAGITTARIUS, MOON AQUARIUS: Unusual and fascinating, well-read and knowledgeable. Stubborn, eccentric and intractable. May preach tolerance, but can be the most intolerant of people.

SUN SAGITTARIUS, MOON PISCES: Caring, spiritual and soft-hearted. Often unrealistic, with little or no interest in the practicalities of life. Lacking in self-esteem and downtrodden.

SUN CAPRICORN, MOON ARIES: Determined, intelligent, forceful and often ruthlessly ambitious. Callous and cold. Anyone who gets in the way of their climb to the top should watch out.

SUN CAPRICORN, MOON TAURUS: Dependable, artistic and down-to-earth. A good homemaker and manager. Can be obstinate and intolerant, hating change or upheaval.

SUN CAPRICORN, MOON GEMINI: Good with words, and excellent at communicating generally, seeing projects through to the end. Can be glib, superficial and occasionally slapdash.

SUN CAPRICORN, MOON CANCER: Faithful, family-centred, with shining integrity. A terrible worrier, given to sulking and brooding over what are often imaginary problems.

SUN CAPRICORN, MOON LEO: Tough, purposeful and ambitious, though can sometimes reveal a surprisingly sympathetic streak. Sometimes secretly soft-hearted. Conversely, can be arrogant and cruel.

SUN CAPRICORN, MOON VIRGO: Business-like, serious, dependable and usually very thorough. Can be pompous and sometimes heavy-going company. Old before their time.

SUN CAPRICORN, MOON LIBRA: Good mixer and motivator, though impractical. Innovative thinker and pioneer. Sometimes gullible and a bit childish.

SUN CAPRICORN, MOON SCORPIO: Strong and determined, with a sense of personal destiny. Can be kind and caring but also sarcastic and too quick to demolish others verbally.

SUN CAPRICORN, MOON SAGITTARIUS: Focused and dedicated, stable, organized and communicative. Need to relax, have more fun and take life a lot easier. Can suffer early burnout.

SUN CAPRICORN, MOON CAPRICORN: Hard workers, with great stamina and powers of endurance. Sympathetic and caring. Uncomfortable with emotion and far too tense. Need to take more time out.

SUN CAPRICORN, MOON AQUARIUS: Efficient, broad-minded and organized, with high standards for themselves and others. Do not suffer fools gladly and can be very intolerant towards those with different lifestyles or views.

SUN CAPRICORN, MOON PISCES: Dedicated, caring and compassionate. Often intuitive with a tendency to have significant dreams. Can be over-sensitive and easily hurt. Should put themselves first occasionally.

SUN AQUARIUS, MOON ARIES: Amusing, energetic and innovative. Often highly motivated but sometimes rather difficult and arrogant. They can sometimes come over as quirky and a little odd.

SUN AQUARIUS, MOON TAURUS: Dogged and dependable. High fliers who often have a marked artistic streak. Obstinate and grumpy, and inclined to get bogged down in the most boring of details.

SUN AQUARIUS, MOON GEMINI: Quick-witted and intelligent. Good communicators. Can be rather flippant and shallow. Occasionally insensitive to the needs and feelings of others.

SUN AQUARIUS, MOON CANCER: Caring and loving, companionable and amusing. Moody and unpredictable. Good at empathizing with others.

SUN AQUARIUS, MOON LEO: Active and busy, purposeful and frequently highly ambitious. Natural loners who are sometimes socially inept, though still keen to make a good impression.

SUN AQUARIUS, MOON VIRGO: Scholarly and intelligent. A dogged researcher. Often seen as a bit of an oddball. Rather awkward, old-fashioned and fussy. Loyal to people and causes.

SUN AQUARIUS, MOON LIBRA: Fun, extrovert, attractive and often rather charming. Can be superficial and lacking focus and stamina. Good with people and animals.

SUN AQUARIUS, MOON SCORPIO: Natural leaders, teachers or gurus. Bright and innovative, and take easily to the centre stage. Underneath the charisma lurks impatience and arrogance.

SUN AQUARIUS, MOON SAGITTARIUS: Clever, bright, impulsive and enthusiastic. Sometimes over-optimistic and unrealistic. Not good with money or planning for a rainy day.

SUN AQUARIUS, MOON CAPRICORN: Business-like and naturally protective of their family. Usually very efficient, though too serious and inclined to worry. Need to realize that life is not always hard.

SUN AQUARIUS, MOON AQUARIUS: Idealistic and broad-minded, with unusual ideas, beliefs and even lifestyle. Usually tough on themselves and others. Can lack real warmth.

SUN AQUARIUS, MOON PISCES: Intuitive, spiritual, caring and often very clever, though impractical. They can have a tendency to be too other-worldly and unfocused. They can also be naive and gullible.

SUN PISCES, MOON ARIES: Intelligent, quick-witted, purposeful and entertaining. Egocentric and occasionally manipulative and emotionally demanding. May even resort to moral blackmail.

SUN PISCES, MOON TAURUS: Musical, harmonious, kind and gregarious. Can be indolent and lacking in motivation and ambition. Easy-going.

SUN PISCES, MOON GEMINI: Quick, bright, spontaneous and amusing. Good company but tend to be anxious and emotionally insecure. All too often in love with love.

SUN PISCES, MOON CANCER: Caring, sympathetic, sensitive and helpful. Good in a crisis, though usually too dreamy and impractical, leaving decisions to others.

SUN PISCES, MOON LEO: Expansive, encouraging, artistic and compassionate. Often egocentric and arrogant. Petulant if crossed. Depressed by bad luck more than most.

SUN PISCES, MOON VIRGO: Profound, psychic and often very creative. Tend to be nervy, obsessive and somewhat weak-willed. Will seek refuge and peace when life gets too tough.

SUN PISCES, MOON LIBRA: Active, innovative, energetic and enthusiastic. Charismatic and good with people. Can inspire and motivate others, but tend to be unrealistic and lacking in stamina.

SUN PISCES, MOON SCORPIO: Compassionate, profound, psychic and often powerful in their chosen field. Unpredictable and occasionally inclined to depression.

SUN PISCES, MOON SAGITTARIUS: Restless, with itchy feet. Great travellers. Often deep and studious, with questing minds. Also unreliable and over-optimistic. Bad planners.

SUN PISCES, MOON CAPRICORN: Intuitive, creative and efficient. Very reliable and solid, with artistic leanings. Tend to be insecure and sometimes lack ambition.

SUN PISCES, MOON AQUARIUS: Open and honest, spiritual and caring. Often have very good ideas. Too otherworldly and 'fey', and inclined to gullibility. Best to keep their feet on the ground.

SUN PISCES, MOON PISCES: Spiritual and mystical, imaginative and intuitive. May have important and powerful dreams. Often lacking in ambition and motivation, and may be somewhat gullible. May suffer from erratic energy levels.

The Moon In Aries

This Moon Sign is all energy and impulsiveness. The Arian tendency to rush in where angels fear to tread is enhanced by the Moon's emotionality, so here we have the great movers and shakers of the world.

Moon in Aries people tend to feel affronted by social injustice. They want the world to be a better place right now, and can become very upset when faced with intractable problems and the slow pace of change. Characteristically, they find it almost impossible to understand opposing views, or even to comprehend that others have a right to express them.

They have charm, wit and an infectious optimism that may not always be justified. These people have original minds and can be very creative if given enough freedom to express themselves. Lunar Arians are more sympathetic and broad-minded than their Sun Sign counterparts.

RELATIONSHIPS

Lunar Arians have no time for whiners or whingers. They react best to practical problems, leaving others to deal with the emotional trauma. Their constant need to get up and go often masks a fear of emotional commitment. They may unconsciously seek partners who are steady homebodies in order to compensate for their own fiery temperament. Then, they will expect their home to be a haven. They expect to be given unconditional love and support, while also demanding unequivocal independence. For the most part they are good and creative with money, although sometimes their moneymaking schemes can prove overly ambitious.

The Moon In Taurus 

Lunar Taureans are emotionally stable and physically strong. These people are happy with their place on Earth, and, even if their lives are difficult, they will endure the vagaries of their lot without any complaint. They find great enjoyment in the good things of life. However, they are not naturally assertive, and prefer to go with the flow rather than make things happen. They are conservative and admire the status quo, but if what they hold dear is challenged, they will muster all their considerable strength to preserve it.

Lunar Taureans often felt they had to keep their thoughts and feelings to themselves as children, and this tendency spills over into adulthood. They feel things deeply, even though they find it almost impossible to say so. Unfortunately, they usually manage to rage at inappropriate moments, bewildering and frightening those around them.

RELATIONSHIPS

Moon in Taurus people are among the least promiscuous of all the zodiac. They are solid, dependable types who see relationships as life commitments and are wary of jumping in headfirst without any thought for the future. When challenged in love, they can become very distressed. They tend not to fight, but retreat hurt.

Socially, Lunar Taureans may be stolid and unimaginative, but they make sensual lovers and can be attracted to more fiery characters, at times to their own detriment. When they do eventually find true love, though, reliable and practical Lunar Taureans make excellent providers for their families and homemakers.

The Moon In Gemini

Lunar Geminians are nervy and witty. There is also a profound underlying restlessness in this Moon placement, as if they feel their skin doesn't fit. An inner conflict often drives them to achieve great things but can also provoke bursts of extreme irritability and bouts of depression.

This Moon Sign cares passionately about promoting themselves and their ego: these people package themselves like a commercial commodity. Words are their natural medium and Lunar Geminians can talk for hours. Although their wordplay can amuse, they can also use words as weapons against others. The Moon gives added depth to this sign: these people can be profound thinkers.

Although prone to changeable moods, dark nights of the soul can ultimately be very creative, allowing them to dredge from the depths of their unconscious the solution to their current predicament.

RELATIONSHIPS

In relationships, Moon Sign Geminians can be irritable, very often feeling trapped and held against their will. Many take a long time to commit themselves emotionally. They may appear flirtatious and sexual, but the truth is that many of them prefer to think and talk about sex rather than do it. Sometimes, it is enough for them to know that they are desired. This is a Peter Pan sign, full of children who never grow up. Consequently, as parents, they can be found thinking up games and bedtime stories until even the most energetic small children get tired.

The Moon In Cancer 

Lunar Cancerians are plagued by their extreme sensitivity. They are compassionate and react strongly to any hint of unhappiness, instantly becoming the valiant protector and carer, although often at great cost to their own peace of mind, because Lunar Cancerians are obsessive worriers.

It is said that their moods change as often as the tides, which, as they are ruled by the Moon, is an apt comparison. Their tendency to be sentimental can prevent them from understanding their moods completely. Unfortunately, Lunar Cancerians can be inveterate sulkers and expect to be cajoled out of their moods.

Not just hoarders of mementos, they hoard people, or rather their memories of them, too. They will not let go, and can wave the fairy wand of wish-fulfilment over reality until it becomes something else entirely.

RELATIONSHIPS

Men and women of this Moon placement have a strong desire to create a nest and are willing to tackle the hard work of creating it themselves. They will, however, expect those around them to acknowledge their efforts and be grateful. Great martyrs, they will nurture grievances for many years.

Lunar Cancerians are in touch with their senses and make extremely good lovers. By nature they are loyal – often to a fault – and so tend to keep partners for life, because of their sheer dedication to making the relationship work.

The Moon In Leo

Moon Sign Leos are generous, noble and encouraging. They are natural leaders who exude drive, and are often protective towards more timid mortals.

They set remarkably high standards for themselves and others, which can lead to all manner of problems. They tend to have a very elevated image of themselves as the most moral people. If the image slips and they experience jealousy, infidelity or dishonesty, they become angry at themselves and everyone around them.

They are very proud of maintaining the status quo and have little time for rebels. They long for excitement, including sexual thrills, and may seek situations where they can show off their mastery – in relationships, in their careers or in dangerous sports. If there is any chance that a specific course of action will make them powerful, they will follow it, however dangerous.

RELATIONSHIPS

Lunar Leos are very romantic. In return, they expect loyalty and support. They will go to almost any lengths for those they love, but they can become extremely hurt if their generosity is rejected.

They are passionate lovers, and adore the idea of romantic involvement. However, their inner restlessness gives them a wandering eye. They can put up with a less-than-perfect relationship for a surprisingly long time, often because they feel that it is the decent thing to do.

They can be overbearing parents and difficult siblings, although often their innate charm will help restore their popularity.

The Moon In Virgo

Sociable and dutiful, Moon Sign Virgoans are the commentators of life. They operate from the shadows, seldom seeking the spotlight but analyzing and observing and, for the moment, saying little. Yet there is an essential paradox in both Solar and Lunar Virgoans. They have all the makings of dullness, but many are charming, with surprisingly exciting views.

They are by nature self-effacing, although if they decide they want to shine, they do so with great panache. Most of the time, though, Lunar Virgoans are content to take a back seat and concern themselves with the daily minutiae of life. They are keen on details.

Mercury, their ruling planet, makes them excellent communicators. They are stalwart friends and colleagues, with a strong code of ethics. They may be messy in their surroundings but their thought processes are almost inevitably tidy.

RELATIONSHIPS

Emotionally, Virgoans are often said to be cold fish, but this is seldom the case beyond a superficial level. Their reserve can give the impression that they are passionless, but, like still waters, their feelings actually run very deep, though it can be hard for them to express them. They are often in great demand as friends, but it can come as something of a shock when their friends discover that they have their failings, too. They can easily descend from easy fellowship into black depression. Like many naturally reserved people, they can often feel secretly hard done by.

The Moon In Libra

Moon Sign Librans are charming, urbane and creative. They seek both harmony and excitement – which can lead to a certain amount of inner tension and contrariness in their behaviour patterns. Libra is a cardinal sign, which adds vibrancy and stamina to the slower, more intuitive characteristics of the Moon in this zodiacal position. Although they may have more than their fair share of leadership qualities, they often prefer to take a back seat and let others take the responsibility.

Lunar Librans often find themselves in the role of peacemakers, which they fulfil admirably. They can see all round a problem and are unusually perceptive about its underlying causes. However, they are able to maintain an objective viewpoint, although under that impartial exterior lies the ability to speak passionately on deeply held views and to hatch plots against those who present obstacles.

RELATIONSHIPS

Moon Sign Librans are often in love with love and throw themselves wholeheartedly into the chase. They cool off, though, once a relationship is established. Although they tend to be hypercritical, they are not as difficult to live with as this might suggest. On the contrary, they can be very loving partners. They are caring and excellent in a crisis. As the sign of the scales, they cannot abide a tense atmosphere and will go out of their way to smooth over ruffled feathers, even if it means compromising their own position. However, this certainly does not mean that they are pushovers.

The Moon In Scorpio

Moon Sign Scorpians are competitive, compelling and sexually inclined. They seek all sorts of excitement, while at the same time appreciating a stable life. There is usually an element of the contradictory in these people, which adds to their unfathomability. This is a potent placement – for good or evil.

Often hard to understand, Lunar Scorpians tend to hide their true feelings and sensitivity under a somewhat hard exterior.

The positive side of their psychic awareness is a well-honed intuition about insincere people. They have the enviable ability to bounce back after personal disaster. Lunar Scorpians are perhaps more caring than the Solar kind, and they are attached to home and family in an almost Cancerian way. They are also fiercely protective, going to great lengths to help those less fortunate than they are.

RELATIONSHIPS

The Moon in Water Signs always make for great emotionality. Moon Sign Scorpians have great difficulty when it comes to expressing their feelings. They can be markedly demanding, but rapidly distance themselves from those they regard as 'clingers'. They like an element of danger in their relationships. They will also provoke inflammatory situations at home just to keep the edge of danger nicely sharpened. They are very sensitive and can easily be persuaded to see another's point of view. They are easily hurt if accused of being in any way unjust or uncaring.

The Moon In Sagittarius

Moon Sign Sagittarians are courageous, intellectually inquisitive and very free spirited. Highly adaptable, they are made for action and are innately gregarious, with a wide circle of admiring friends. They have clear minds and are able to cut through unnecessary detail to the central issue.

In their love lives, Lunar Sagittarians hate to be tied down, either physically or intellectually. These are not power-hungry people, nor are they money-mad or particularly fond of competition.

Traditionally, this Moon placement has few serious faults, but can live very much in a world of its own, always optimistic that things will turn out all right in the end. Moon Sign Sagittarians are, to some degree, less outgoing than their Solar counterparts, but they still possess the same basic desire to like and be liked by everyone they meet.

RELATIONSHIPS

Lunar Sagittarians may find problems with close relationships. They tend to make a distinction between sexual passion and the gentler sort of unconditional love – although their partners may not see it in quite the same way. Lunar Sagittarians are often more attracted to the idea of sexual encounters than to the act itself.

They often talk big, persuading people that they are high-fliers, but do nothing to make their dreams become reality. At its most negatively aspected, this Moon placement creates fantasists. However, their tall tales are not deliberate manipulations – they often believe them themselves.

The Moon In Capricorn

Moon Sign Capricornians are serious, dependable and controlled. Very practical people, they do not shirk responsibility and have great foresight. Sensitive and refined by nature, they may seem slightly old-fashioned, but can adapt surprisingly well to new situations. They tend to be reserved and somewhat shy when young, but gradually develop an outward sophistication.

Lunar Capricornians tend to plan their futures when others are still more interested in playground games. Their ruler Saturn bestows very mixed blessings: they are expected to take life seriously right from the cradle.

All Capricornians have acquired an unfair reputation as pessimists plagued with bad luck. In fact, Saturn gives them a great deal of wisdom – which can bestow old heads on young shoulders – and the chance to develop spiritually well beyond the usual opportunities granted to most people.

RELATIONSHIPS

Under their wise, cautious image, Lunar Capricornians hide a great deal of sensitivity – more so than their Sun Sign counterparts. However, they learn early in life to keep their feelings under control. They are very uncomfortable with any kind of emotional scene, though deep down inside they may be crying out in sympathy.

They are slow to give their hearts, even in friendship, but once committed to a relationship will honour it through thick and thin. It is important to them to have security, both emotional and financial. They are wonderful providers and protectors.

The Moon In Aquarius

Moon Sign Aquarians are cool, broad-minded, humanitarian and optimistic. They are idealists with high personal standards, and their strongly developed sense of independence means that they rarely become a burden to others, either financially or emotionally.

Forward-looking and optimistic, they embrace the future with enthusiasm. They also have a tendency to be too eager to abandon old ways of doing things, and the traditions that have become hallowed by age; and they can be very insensitive to those who still uphold them.

On the whole, however, Lunar Aquarians are easy-going, congenial folk who attract a wide range of friends and lovers. Sexually, they can be romantic, passionate and – being a Fixed sign – very loyal, even to partners who repeatedly let them down. Aquarians, both Solar and Lunar, rarely sulk or brood, being far too busy with a hundred and one plans and schemes.

RELATIONSHIPS

It is essential for Lunar Aquarians to find a life partner who shares their interests. Aquarians desperately need to stay in their own niche, and anyone who is uncomfortable with that will not last the course.

Aquarians operate from the premise that they know what is best and have the only valid interpretation of events; others had better do things their way or get out. Lunar Aquarians tend to have big egos no matter how gentle they may seem. For once, the Moon has the effect of diminishing emotionality, and this can help create some very cool customers indeed.

The Moon In Pisces

Moon Sign Pisceans are emotional, kind and creative. Soft-hearted and vulnerable, this Moon placement cannot bear disharmony, and works hard to eliminate all upsets – real, potential or imagined! They instinctively reach out to others, and may even sacrifice their own wellbeing in order to help and support those around them. This can escalate to a very unhealthy degree: many become uncomplaining, downtrodden martyrs who harbour secret resentments for years.

Lunar Pisceans are the psychics of the zodiac, picking up information about people and places at a profound, often inexplicable, level. They are also the greatest worriers of the zodiac. They constantly fret about their nearest and dearest, but also spend valuable time worrying about the state of the world. Unfortunately, by their very nature these particular problems are intractable, adding to the burden of Lunar Piscean worry.

RELATIONSHIPS

Lunar Pisceans are seldom content to live alone. They see their own worth in terms of how much they are loved by others, not understanding that they themselves need to love just as much, if not more. But if the reality of love never quite matches up to their romantic expectations, they are happy to make believe, living in a world of illusion. The presence of their co-ruler Neptune encourages escapism, which can become a serious threat to their mental wellbeing.

Sexually, Lunar Pisceans are eager, sensuous and imaginative. They detest being ridiculed or humiliated.

Online Resources:

Sun sign calculator:

https://www.lunarium.co.uk/calendar/universal.jsp

https://cafeastrology.com/whats-my-sun-sign.html

http://www.astrosage.com/sunsign.asp

Moon sign calculator:

https://www.astrocal.co.uk/moon-sign-calculator/

https://cafeastrology.com/whats-my-moon-sign.html

https://astrolibrary.org/moon-sign-calculator/

Love compatibility calculator:

https://horoscopes.astro-seek.com/love-compatibility-calculator-horoscope-matching

http://www.mylovecal.com

https://www.sevenreflections.com/lovecalculator/

How to find your vocation in the horoscope

https://www.astro.com/info/in_vocation2_e.htm

http://www.psychicscoop.com/career-indicators-horoscope

https://www.horoscope.com/us/horoscopes/career/index-horoscope-career-daily.aspx

Daily Horoscope:

https://www.astrology.com/horoscopes.html

https://cafeastrology.com/sundailyhoroscopes.html

http://www.astrocenter.com/us/horoscope-daily-index.aspx?Af=0